11·18·14

Hi Bluetiful,

Thank you so much for supporting my memoir. While I was hand delivered this, please sent with ALOTTA love. you appreciate you! Hope you love my story.

- love,
Danny

JOY JUICE

A young man's story
about chemo, cancer
& good fortune

✳

by Daniel Alotta

Copyright © 2013 by Daniel Alotta

Joy Juice
by Daniel Alotta

Printed in the United States of America
PMDJ Press

ISBN: 978-0-9897504-0-0

All rights reserved solely by the author. The author guarantees all
contents are original and do not infringe upon the legal rights of
any other person or work. No part of this book may be reproduced
in any form without the permission of the author. The views
expressed in this book are not necessarily those of the publisher.

Book design by Christina Newhard (www.newharddesign.com).
Cover illustration/logo design by Jon Deus (www.descript.me).

This book is dedicated to

Dr. Mark Brower,
in loving memory,

and

my Mom and Pop.
You dedicated your lives
to making sure I'd keep mine.
I love you!

Table of Contents

Prologue 1

HS Essay 2

Sonogram 7

CAT Scan 15

Dr. Brower. 19

Bone Marrow Test 22

The Waiting. 27

Biopsy. 32

More Waiting. 36

Game Plan. 37

Me and My Pop. 40

The Sperm Bank 42

Joy Juice 47

The Tidy Bowl Man. 51

My Pills. 57

Chemo 60

H & H. 72

Bad Hair Day. 75

Side Effects 76

First Day of School 82

My Sister. 87

Dr. B's Office. 91

Game Time 93

Tube Talk. 98

Alien Inside Me. 102

Table of Contents

Pillow Talk. 103

Post Op. 105

Phantom Cells 108

Remission/College/Getting Back in Shape. . . 109

Temple University 112

Lingering Effects 125

"Danny, You're Cured" 128

Chemo-power. 133

Sperm Bank Revisited 134

Cancer Beyond Being Cured 135

Reflection/Epilogue 136

Acknowledgements 139

Prologue

Survivor.... Such an interesting word. When I meet people that don't know my story and they find out, they often say something to the effect like "Wow, you beat it!" or "Man, that's incredible! You're a Survivor!" Despite the fact that that's true and I did survive, the truth is I didn't beat it. Make no mistake, it let me live. Yes I had what was considered a good attitude and everyone said I fought valiantly, but the word Survivor to me, implies that I did something that someone else in my shoes that passed away didn't do. If "making it" or "surviving" is that something, I certainly didn't do that or miraculously will it. I've known other people who were stricken with cancer that had the same will to live as I did and unfortunately didn't make it.

When I was a young boy my grandfather died of lung cancer. I don't remember him a great deal but I know from my mom's stories that he had a zest for life. He had a great family with three young grandchildren and every reason to want to live yet he didn't. Then there was my cousin Marvin, who always worked out, played sports and never smoked a day in his life, yet he too died of lung cancer. With the birth of his first grandchild Maddy, occurring shortly before he was diagnosed, he had everything to live for and he was still taken from us. Both my grandpa and cousin wanted to live and they didn't get the chance.

Is the word Survivor really trying to tell me that I did something that all those that lost their fight didn't do? No. No way, I'm not buying it. Myself and every other *survivor* are actually members of a different category. We are the *Fortunate's!* No matter how difficult the road someone has had to endure, no matter how many operations, rounds of radiation or chemo, the fact remains if you endure you were fortunate to be given far better circumstances then the countless people we have lost to this monster. The next time someone calls you a survivor, set the record straight and tell them you are a **Fortunate.**

HS Essay

I covered myself with a blanket to keep warm against the winter cold. I had been sleeping but was interrupted by the sounds of someone crying. Though the tears fell as if part of a torrential rainstorm, I was able to hear each individual drop fall as they formed a pool of sorrow. Pit pat. Pit pat.

These sounds were coming from my mother's room. Why was she crying uncontrollably? Damn! It was obvious. The doctor must have phoned with the results of my biopsy. I felt trapped. After several days the waiting was over. My worst fears were about to be realized. I must be dying. Why else would my mother be so hysterical? The most awful thoughts pierced through me. The doctors had made a definite diagnosis. I had cancer and it was fatal.

With these thoughts of my demise running through my head, I felt trapped. "God, I don't know if you're listening, but I don't think I'm ready to die. I mean…"

At that moment, I could hear each footstep as my mom walked down the hallway towards the living room. Just before she entered, I became fixated on her shadow which was now painted on the wall. As I lay on the couch, a cold sweat formed on my brow. Sweat began to drip into my eyes blurring my vision as I did my best to focus on this image until it became an actual presence in front of me.

My mother's limp body stood there, face puffy and red from crying. My throat parched, I gulped for moisture and my voice trembled when I asked, "Am I dying?" Hearing me say those words rocked my mom like nothing I had ever seen causing her tears to intensify and it seemed like she began choking on her own breath.

The next few seconds seemed like an eternity. "Just the opposite sweetheart" she cried. "You have Hodgkin's Disease. You are going to live!"

Then why are you crying?

Because I'm so happy!

At seventeen, this was all pretty confusing as I don't know if I had ever witnessed tears of joy before. Well let me be clear, they're amazingly powerful. My mom embraced me and we hugged for what seemed like a frozen moment. It was frigid outside that day and there was frost on the window but the warmth in the room was so intense nothing could have penetrated it. Sunlight filled the room in which we sat. We were quiet. This was our moment. A mother and her son... I might have been seventeen but I was still her baby and we had just been given a second chance.

That was my senior year of high school and it would prove to be unforgettable as a senior year should. However, it all started as routinely as any other teenage boy's senior year with raging hormones. I couldn't get enough of my girlfriend, I played on three teams and my friends and I were all getting ready for the SAT's. Those were my priorities and most likely in that order. School itself... Well it was just that. Who could focus? It was early fall and the weather was still magnificent. With the exception of my English teacher, everything was dandy.

Ah, my English teacher. At the time, in my world she was possibly the meanest cusp in existence. Every day, the heat in her classroom was turned up to the max yet she refused to open the windows. Being as though my last name began with an A, I had the first seat by the door and I'd usually open it slightly for some fresh air only to have her slam it shut. It was a never ending back and forth. Unable to cope with the heat, I'd eventually fall asleep and like clockwork she would call on me as soon as I did. My friends would crack up at this daily charade. Whether coincidence or not, I always seemed to be tired in English class.

One afternoon I exhibited similar fatigue at tennis practice and my coach asked if everything was alright as I was usually extremely energetic. With the invincibility of youth on my side, I shrugged it off as nothing and proceeded to push harder. After all, a little fatigue was nothing to think twice about. It was no different than being hungry for a mid day snack. It happened all the time. You dealt with it and moved on. No big deal.

However, this lack of energy seemed to present itself regularly at irregular times. It was one thing to get tired during class but it continued to show itself at practice and even while hanging out with friends. There would be times when I would keel over from discomfort in my mid section but I was always getting bumped around during my hockey games. At the end of the day, who had time to pay it any mind? Blessed with the beautiful arrogance of youth, I believed I was unstoppable.

That all changed as my first major rowing competition approached and the signs of a strong cold began to show itself. I had a slight fever and white spots on my tonsils. My mom happened to have a Z-pack (Zithromax) handy and we self medicated so that I'd be able to compete and compete I did. I had done incredibly well in my first race as a member of an elite team in New York City and defeated my cold in one fell swoop. Despite my race being over, little did I know my cold was still in a competition of its own and as soon as I finished my Z-pack a clear winner was determined.

A few days after I finished my meds, I woke up with a 104 degree temperature. I quickly learned this was no ordinary flu! I could barely walk ten feet without having to sit down. Every task no matter how minor required inordinate amounts of energy to complete. Brushing my teeth, had to sit down. Trying to walk from my bedroom to the kitchen, had to sit down. Even urinating was too grave a task and again I had to sit down. Every night like clockwork I sweat through another set of sheets.

In my house getting a cold was no big deal, you got over it. For some reason, this one didn't seem to let up. Back then we lived on a tree lined street in Jackson Heights, Queens. Growing up, my building and block served as an extended family. Between my building and the one next door, there were a dozen kids all within my age range so there was always someone to play sports with, ride bikes or get into some form of mischief. Amongst that group was my big sister, who at three and a half years older than me, could play sports as well as any of us. When I started baseball around the age of five, I was absolutely the original Bad News Bear. With her help and constant practice, by year two I went from not being able to hit the ball to what seemed like not missing it. You couldn't keep me indoors. I wanted to be outside from the time the sun rose till after the street lights came on. As long as I was in the fresh air playing, I don't think I even needed food.

My mom and dad were great and having grown up in the Bronx and Brooklyn respectively they understood and could relate to the desire to play on the block all day long. As a kid in New York City, "The Block" or "The Stoop" is part of your culture. We created and played games like "Stoop Ball" or "Over the Wire," which my cousins in the suburbs never heard of. Yet amongst my peers, they were the games through which you built a reputation.

My parents, sister and I were all extremely close. Other than one set of cousins on each side of the family, we didn't have a large extended family so we grew up spending quality time with one another. Perhaps our favorite thing to do together was cook. Whether it was cutting garlic or parsley, my sister and I often served as the apprentices in the kitchen. Our favorite role was undoubtedly taste tester, especially when dad was making tomato sauce. My sister and I couldn't get enough and we would often eat multiple bowls of sauce prior to our meal.

Being so close, when I got my flu it was something that everyone was concerned about. Upon calling my doctor, he explained that a bad strain of influenza was going around and that we should give it a few more days. A few more days came and went without progress and my dad lost patience with the give it some time approach. After all, I had been no stranger to colds and flus as a child having had pneumonia and bronchitis several times growing up. This time around he knew in his gut something was different. When we phoned my doctor again he insisted that he see me which he did that afternoon.

While performing my physical examination we ran the gamut of checking my eyes, ears, nose, temperature and glands. However, it was upon examining my torso when my doctor asked me if I had ever gotten a sonogram a year earlier. Almost a year to the day prior I had torn a section of my abdomen while training which as a result caused internal bleeding and intense pain. At the time he explained if the pain didn't go away within a week I would need a sonogram.

Luckily the pain went away in five days. Was this Fortunate? We'll get back to this.

No sooner than I had responded to this question did my doctor walk over to the phone on the wall and place a call. It was the end of the work day and I was his last patient. Once someone picked up he began ordering an immediate sonogram but based upon his responses it was clear that all the technicians had gone home for the day. He then explained to the person on the other end that regardless of their calendar the following day that I would be their first patient. In everyone's life there are certain moments that you never forget. For me, this is one of those moments. I vividly remember Dr. Goldberg hanging up the phone.

When he turned to talk to me, he had a look on his face of a father about to give his son bad news. Dr. Goldberg wasn't just a doctor. He truly cared. He had always been very genuine with my parents and they trusted him explicitly. Knowing him however, I'm certain he had that type of relationship with many of his patients. Yet he made you feel as if you were the only one that mattered. When he finally spoke, he said I was scheduled for a sonogram the following morning. He hadn't said anything to cause alarm and I know he didn't mean to be so expressive but it was clear through his delivery he knew something wasn't right and it weighed on him. For some reason, at that moment I said to myself "I have cancer."

Where did that thought even come from? It made no sense. I was by far the fittest in my family. I played sports every day and ate more fruits and vegetables than anyone you had ever seen. My mom often joked that she thought I was going to turn into an orange as it was nothing for me to eat six, eight or even ten in one sitting. When it came to berries I would eat at least a box at a time. As soon as any fruit was purchased I ate them. So how then was it possible that I could be sick?

Once we finished in the examination room, Dr. Goldberg had me get dressed and return to his office where both he and my parents awaited. It was then he explained to my parents what I had already learned. It was at that instant I realized how distinctly different parents and children digest the same news. Despite my inner thought of having cancer, I had brushed it off as if it were as simple as pouring a glass of juice in the morning. This is truly one of the joys of being seventeen. Ignorance is absolutely bliss.

The mere word nearly shot my mom out of her chair.

Sonogram???!!!

Why does he need a sonogram?

Dr. Goldberg's attempts to calm my mom down were futile. With each attempt her nervousness grew. He explained that "We're simply trying to understand what's going on." This wasn't good enough.

What are we looking for?

What's so wrong that he needs a sonogram?

It took a ton to get my mom to calm down. Even when she finally did you knew she wanted to ask more questions but she held back. I learned that day that not having direct answers to a parent's questions actually torments them. Instead, they had their imaginations wondering the worst. When we left Dr. Goldberg's office that afternoon I could tell my folks were uneasy. My mom repeatedly asked me what Dr. Goldberg had said to me during my physical. "What else" she kept saying as if somehow by continuing to ask she could uncover additional information which I didn't have. I didn't dare tell them of my earlier thought from the examination room.

Sonogram

The following morning the three of us readied ourselves for our appointment. I sat on the stoop while my mom and I waited for my dad to bring the car around. My inner thoughts from the previous day seemed to hang over me. As my dad pulled up I jokingly said to my mom "Watch, I probably have cancer." Somehow it seemed by casually joking about it, the possibility would evaporate. My mother on the other hand was not too amused.

Why would you say such a thing?

Don't even think such craziness.

When my parents and I showed up at East River Imaging for my sonogram, my dad dropped us off so that he could go to work for a quick spell and pick us up when we were finished. He was in the restaurant business and had just opened a new place in the Chelsea section of Manhattan almost exactly the same time as when I came down with my flu. Despite the fact that I would see my dad shortly, when he and I hugged each other good bye I could feel him take a deep breath as if he was praying and hugging me at the same time. There are certain feelings that are unmistakable and this was one of them.

After my mom filled out a bunch of forms we waited for a technician to call my name. Within a few minutes it was time.

Daniel Alotta?

Yes.

Come with me please.

My fever at this point was still 104 and I was extremely weak. I sluggishly followed the technician into the examination room. He was a friendly chap and even asked how I was feeling. I explained that I had been better but overall I had no complaints. Once we got set up, we were ready to go. This was my first sonogram and I was unaware that both the gel and wand could actually be quite cold. Once I got past that, it was a piece of cake. The technician began to... well let's just say he technician-ed.

Within a few minutes he began to focus on the left side of my abdomen. He stayed on this side for what seemed like ten to fifteen minutes. Finally I asked him what he was looking at and his response was "Your spleen." Not to be completely ignorant, but at seventeen not only didn't I know what a spleen was, I don't even think I knew I had one. Isn't ignorance grand? The technician began to explain that my spleen was the organ that filtered toxins from the blood. I couldn't help but think "Yeah, so? What does that have to do with me?" Apparently at that moment a great deal. My spleen which the technician informed me was supposed to be the size of a small breakfast sausage, was nearly two and a half to three footballs in size. Now I may not have known what a spleen was or that I even had one, but I didn't have to be a genius to recognize that this was no bueno.

I asked him what that meant and he wouldn't say much but he didn't have to.

Unbeknownst to me, while my sonogram was taking place, Dr. Katz, the doctor in charge of reading my images not only had been doing so but he had already contacted Dr. Goldberg and proceeded to call my mother into his office while my test was ongoing. As he began showing her my images that were lit up on the wall, she immediately asked if everything was alright. "Unfortunately no" he responded. My mom can be extremely emotional and hearing these words caused her to grab the leather chair closest to her. Before she could catch her breath and utter a word Dr. Katz told her he believed I had lymphoma. And there it was. My strange gut feeling from the day before had come true.

My mom told me she nearly ripped the leather chair with her nails when she heard the news.

Lymphoma! She cried out.

But…but…that's cancer!!!

It is. Dr. Katz replied.

"How is this possible?" my mom pleaded with the doctor. Unfortunately, this is the one question he couldn't answer. Dr. Katz proceeded to tell my mom that he believed my cancer to be pretty advanced and that she should pray for it to be Hodgkin's Disease, which they knew a great deal about and had tremendous success with thus increasing my chances to live. Hodgkin's is a form of lymphoma which causes your lymph glands which we have throughout our bodies, to swell. If it were not Hodgkin's my odds would fade drastically. This news hit my mom hard and she could barely stand. In utter disbelief she kept asking questions.

How advanced?

What are you saying?

How is this possible?

Understanding the emotion of the situation, Dr. Katz did his best to calm my mom. He explained that time was critical and that Dr. Goldberg had already been notified and he was waiting for both of us at his office.

Once my mom had done her best to process the news she had just been given, she realized she had to call my dad. Distraught, she had to gather herself enough to call him and deliver the news. When my dad picked up the phone he could sense something was incredibly off.

What's wrong? He demanded.

The mere thought was too much and she couldn't utter the "word." "You have to meet us at Dr. Goldberg's office," was all she could say. Adamant, my dad demanded "What is it? What's wrong?" All my mom could muster was "It's not good. Please hurry."

Hurry he did. Despite being both downtown and across town, my dad beat both me and my mom to Dr. Goldberg's office. Being in the dark he had to know what was happening. My dad is a very old school Sicilian man and at this point all formalities were off the table.

Harvey, what's going on?

Phil, we're pretty sure Danny has lymphoma.

What?

Lymphoma?

What are you saying?

I find it ironic that both my mother and father's reaction were similar. I can only assume that every parent would react with the same disbelief and they would have to be told outright what the circumstances were in order to believe it. Almost as if that one word was a necessary finality.

Phil, were pretty sure Danny has cancer.

There it was. With those three words my Superman found his kryptonite. He took a seat, slumped over and tears began to fall. Very few things could cause my Superman to show such emotion. With his hands over his eyes shielding his tears he was in total disbelief.

I don't understand. How can this be?

Dr. Goldberg attempted to comfort my dad but as you can imagine this was not possible. My dad's world too was crumbling in front of him and there was nothing he could do. Knowing my dad, this is not something he was accustomed to. He's the type of person who believes in making things happen. No matter what, anything is possible. However, right then, at that moment he was left with a circumstance he was unable to influence. He sat there with his heart in his hand as Dr. Goldberg spoke of next steps. Could he even hear the words being spoken to him?

Phil we need to act fast. First thing tomorrow Danny is going to have a CAT scan and then you're going to see Dr. Mark Brower. He's one of the best oncologists around. If Danny were my son, this is the only person I'd send him to. I've already spoken with him and there are no better hands to be in.

Phil???!!!

My dad was in a haze. He could barely comprehend what was happening. "Phil" repeated Dr. Goldberg.

Thank you Harvey, but what about Danny?

Is he going to be ok?

Is he... Is he dying?

The mere thought of his own words sent my dad into an emotional spiral. Ordinarily he would have held strong but there was no room for a facade as he could no longer contain himself and he sobbed right there in front of Dr. Goldberg. Dr. Goldberg did everything he could to console my dad but the truth was still the truth, he couldn't provide all the answers my dad was looking for.

The honest truth is we don't have that information at this point.

What we do know is, whatever it is, it's pretty advanced and like I said, we need to act fast.

While this conversation was taking place I was back at East River Imaging finishing up my sonogram. Once dressed, I rejoined my mom who had returned to the waiting room. How she was able to compose herself without letting on that anything was wrong was nothing short of incredible. Moments earlier she was hysterical yet when I saw her again she was able to greet me in her usual cheerful way. Where did she find this strength? She gave me a hug and we walked outside to get a taxi. I never thought it was strange that we were going to Dr. Goldberg's office as this was my first sonogram so I just took this as the norm.

When my mom and I arrived, the assistant alerted Dr. Goldberg to our presence. When the office intercom rang, my dad was sitting there struggling to control his emotion. "Marlene and Daniel Alotta are here" said the voice in the intercom. There was my pop, a complete wreck and I was practically on the other side of the door.

Phil. Do you need a moment before they come in?

Undoubtedly he did. After gathering himself he let Dr. Goldberg know it was alright to let me and my mom into his office. My dad took one more deep breath. The door opened. My mom and I entered Dr. Goldberg's office. Everyone was privy to what was about to be said, except me. I walked over to my dad to say hello. I remember him hugging me as if he never wanted to let go. I didn't think anything of it as hugs were prized possessions in my family and we always gave them.

At this point all of the events leading up to and including that day were all part of an adventure. I had no idea of the nightmare my parents had just endured. I was just cruising along. When I turned around after hugging my dad, my mom looked teary eyed. In retrospect I would have to believe the <u>site</u> of my dad and me hugging triggered emotion that she was unable to hold back. Then my mom and dad hugged each other as if they had lost something dear to them and couldn't find it. I think they kept their embrace as brief as possible so I wouldn't catch on that anything was wrong.

Similar to the day before, Dr. Goldberg had a tepid look on his face. I didn't know what he was about to say but it was clear that whatever it was weighed on him a bit.

So Danny, Dr. Katz has sent me your sonogram and given me his reading as well.

Your test showed that you probably have lymphoma.

There it was again. With that my mom lost it and started crying hysterically. My dad, clearly affected by what was just said, did his best to keep it together for everyone. And me? I sat there as clueless as clueless can be. Lymophoma? More than anything at this point, I was bewildered.

Uh, ok. What does that mean?

What's lymphoma?

Danny, lymphoma is a form of cancer that affects your lymph glands which you have throughout your body. Typically, when you have cancer they swell. In your case, your sonogram showed that several of your organs including your spleen, kidneys and liver are quite enlarged. At this point I was completely puzzled.

Thinking to myself I wondered...

Cancer?

Me?

I know he's a great doctor, but does he know what he's talking about?
All I have is a bad cold.

Despite telling myself the day before I had cancer, at that moment
the thought made no sense to me and I refused to believe it. I was
healthy. He couldn't be talking about me. There had to be some
confusion, a mistake. They must have mixed up my test with someone
else's. All I had was a cold. A bad cold! If I truly was as sick as he was
saying, what was the difference between having a bad cold and cancer?
Just give me some medicine right? That's all I needed. Dr. Goldberg
realized that I didn't really comprehend the gravity of the situation.

Danny, do you have any more questions?

Uh, I guess?

What exactly does that mean?

Am I dying?

Hearing those words caused my mom to lose it again. Time
seemed to stand still. It was as if multiple scenes of a movie were
being shot at once. I sat in the middle of my folks totally naïve,
having a conversation with my doctor while my folks were having
their own distinct moments. My mom, unable to contain herself on
one side of me while my dad, sat there trying his best to be strong for
everyone on the other side. Everyone was listening intently to what
was being said but clearly processing the outcome in their own way.

Dr. Goldberg explained that at this time we didn't have enough
information and that more tests were needed to determine exactly
what we were dealing with. From there we would be able to establish
a game plan. That truly didn't mean anything to me at the moment
so I pressed him further.

What does that mean?

Firstly, we're sending you for a CAT scan tomorrow.

A CAT scan which stands for Computerized Axial Tomography is a
type of x-ray that uses a computer to generate detailed cross sectional

and 3D views of the body's internal organs and structures. Learning that I needed this test meant nothing to me. My folks on the other hand seemed to intensify with each of Dr. Goldberg's words. I know they wanted to interrupt and ask questions but they let him continue.

After that you have to see Dr. Brower. He's the best and if you were my son, that's who I'd send you to. By the time you see him he'll have the preliminary results of your scan and he'll be able to assess further. Once we do that, we have to find out potentially what kind of cancer we're dealing with. This may seem like a lot, but doing this will allow us to set a course of action.

Regardless of the fact that he basically repeated himself, somehow it made more sense the second time around. In my typical nonchalant fashion I replied.

Okay, sounds good to me.

Despite my casualness, my folks were anything but. They pressed further, asking what exactly we were dealing with despite the fact that they knew the answer before asking the question. It's as if somehow by asking again and again the possibility of getting a definitive answer would reveal itself. Again and again they were greeted with the same ambiguity. The fact remained that they didn't know exactly what was wrong. We would meet Dr. Brower the next morning and start getting to the bottom of this. Dr. Goldberg comforted my folks and explained his door was always open. He was great.

If you need anything, even if you simply need to talk, I'm available.
We're going to do everything we can to get through this.

You knew that he meant his words and they did a great deal to comfort my folks. If ever there was a model for bedside manner Dr. Goldberg was absolutely it. His words truly helped my folks. They left the office that day with a slight sense of comfort they didn't have when they arrived. We all shook Dr. Goldberg's hand on the way out. My dad however, seemed to shake and hold his hand for a few extra minutes. They looked into each other's eyes as if to acknowledge they understood each other and especially the journey that was about to take place.

As we exited the office my dad put his arm around me. None of us quite knew what to say at that moment and both the elevator ride down and car ride home were a bit surreal. There we were, all of us with multiple thoughts running through our minds yet it was eerily quiet. At that moment however, I'm pretty sure my parents were in shock. How could this be happening? What was our road ahead? We were scheduled for more tests and to meet our new doctor the following day. What would he be like? Would he be as compassionate as Dr. Goldberg? What if he gave us more bad news? What if…? So many questions unanswered. Their minds had to be spiraling. As for me…Well, the cold that originally brought me to the doctor in the first place was still kicking my butt. I still had a 104 degree fever and was void of any real energy. The truth was, in general I slept more than anything and the car ride home was no different. Every so often a question regarding how I was feeling would surface and I would look up, open my eyes and utter my usual "fine."

That evening at home was a blur. Between my fever and the day's events I was so tired that I barely remember eating dinner. As usual I passed out on the couch. When I could keep my eyes open, my folks, especially my mom, wanted to know my thoughts about what had happened earlier. She wanted to talk and learn how I was feeling but unfortunately at that moment I truthfully didn't have much to share. The CAT scan was merely a next step and didn't mean anything to me. I could tell it meant a great deal to my folks and despite all their thoughts, I believe they didn't want to alarm or confuse me so they went along with the fact that I didn't want to talk about it.

At some point that evening I was finally peeled from the couch and shown my way to my bedroom. Getting me off the couch had become an "at your own risk" event over the years in my house. Being as though I tossed, turned and even kicked in my sleep it was often safer to just let me be. Ordinarily I was beyond a sound sleeper. I could and had slept through everything and my capacity to do so was often the subject of envy amongst my family. So it was safe to assume, that when I landed in my own bed that I was there to stay and the next time my eyes would open would be the following morning. Customarily that was a smart assumption.

However, in the couple of weeks since my fever had taken hold I would regularly be woken up by my profuse sweating. That night was no different. I don't have the faintest idea what time it was or even how long I had been in the bed. What I do know is that my tossing and turning that night was accompanied by puddles of sweat and shortness of breath. I took a deep breath when I woke, sat up and wiped the sweat off my forehead with my comforter. I was beyond restless.

I searched for the luxury of a dry section of my bed to return to. When I found it at the foot of my bed I reversed my body position and began to resituate myself. As I did I heard the slight sounds of conversation in the distance. I might have been young but I could tell this was no ordinary discussion. My parents were crying. Like a brand in the side of cattle it was a sound that left its impression on me. They were clearly doing their best not to be too loud and under my usual sleeping pattern I would have never heard them. I struggled to get up but it was to no avail, I didn't have the energy. I called for my folks but no sound came out. I took a deep breath and tried calling for them again but my attempt was futile.

Having a 104 degree fever for the better part of two weeks had clearly sapped my energy and at that moment, even the most basic of functions was too demanding. Exhausted, I lay down at the foot of my bed. There may not have been any sounds coming out of my mouth but I began talking to my parents anyway. Somehow I had to let them know everything was going to be alright.

Don't cry Ma!
Don't cry Pop!
I'm going to be ok, you'll see. I promise!
Somehow they heard me right?
I promise I'll be ok.
I promise I'll be ok.
I promise…
I just kept saying it over and over.

The next thing I knew it was morning. I awoke in my sweat soaked bed. When I made it to the kitchen my parents were having their morning coffee. They looked to be up for quite some time. Had they slept? Whether they had or hadn't they greeted me with their usual morning positivity. You see, they always taught me to believe in the power of positive energy and that anything was possible. Whether it was a front to conceal their own angst or completely genuine it helped provide a light mood that morning as it was going to be a long day.

CAT Scan

First stop, we were headed back to East River. Ordinarily I'd have breakfast in the morning. However, you're not allowed to eat prior to getting a CAT scan. I might have been sick but I hadn't lost my appetite so this didn't sit well with me. I proceeded to enjoy my big glass of water. Mmmm!!! By the time we got to East River my stomach wouldn't stop talking. Ahead I had to consume an iodine based solution that helps highlight your organs/insides.

Prior to getting there my mom had spoken with East River about the day's proceedings. There was one major catch. The iodine solution I spoke of earlier gets mixed into a half gallon of cranberry juice which needs to get consumed in the hour prior to the CAT scan. Unfortunately for me I despised cranberry juice. It actually made me sick. My mom had asked if we could bring a bottle of apple juice with us instead but she was told that wasn't an option. So there we were sitting in the waiting room when the receptionist brought out that dreaded bottle of cranberry juice, shook it up one last time and poured out the first glass. Then she said "Ok, you have an hour to finish this."

The mere site of it turned my face sour. My mom offered words of encouragement so I picked up the first cup. As it got close to my nose and I caught the first whiff, I shook my head. This wasn't going to happen. I put the cup back down, took a deep breath and leaned against the wall. All I could think was why couldn't we have brought apple juice with us? Some time passed and my folks urged me to take one sip as it was important. I managed to do so but it wasn't pretty. I know this sounds crazy but cranberry juice truly makes me nauseous.

An hour later when I was supposed to be finished the technician in charge of my CAT scan came out to get me. At that point I had yet to finish 8 ounces of juice. He offered some ice to make it colder and easier to drink. It helped but when he returned 30 minutes later not only had I barely finished one cup but I was so nauseous that I couldn't take anymore. I hadn't done my job and I felt bad about it.

I'm sorry I didn't drink everything but cranberry juice makes me sick.

I'm about to throw up.

I just don't understand why we couldn't bring apple juice with us.

With a puzzled look on his face, my technician replied.

What? Of course you could have.

That was all my mom needed to hear. She lost it. She stormed to the counter to speak with the individual that told her apple juice was not allowed and politely let her have it. You weren't messing with her baby and getting away with it. She actually made the receptionist come from behind the counter and apologize to me. Go Mom!!!

Once apologies were accepted it was time to accompany my technician to the back and get this CAT scan going as we were nearly an hour behind schedule. First you have to change into a robe as you can't have any foreign or metal objects as they interfere with the test. Not sure why but they keep it pretty cold in that room. After lying down, they handed me ear plugs and covered me with blankets to keep warm as the test was going to take an hour or so as they were taking images of my entire torso. Why the earplugs? According to the technician it got pretty noisy in there. Only one way to find out I thought to myself.

As I got comfortable, another person came in and started an intravenous of more iodine. My CAT scan required an additional dosage of iodine, but being as though I never finished the solution it was extra important. I believe they gave me extra since I barely drank any but how much iodine did I need? By the time they were finished pumping me with the stuff I'd be glowing in the dark. My only guess was that they really wanted to know what was going on inside me. Couldn't they tell from all the noise my stomach was making? I was starving! That's what was going on. When the I.V. was in we were ready.

Fortunately I'm not claustrophobic, however, if you are a CAT scan is definitely not for you. Although it varies, in this case I went head first into the tunnel. As I entered, the ceiling and walls seemed to close in on me so I shut my eyes. When I opened them for a brief moment, it would have been easy to develop a fear of tight spaces right then as the ceiling height was only a couple of inches above my eyes. It was extremely dark and the only light available peeked through from each end of the tunnel as if to remind me of a possible escape. I couldn't resist reaching up real quick to touch the ceiling in order to define my boundaries but quickly closed my eyes as soon as I did. Just in case I got to the point where I couldn't take it anymore, I was handed an emergency button that I could press if I needed out of there. It was show time. My technician's voice began talking to me through an intercom explaining that he was going to need me to hold my breath at times. Therefore, there was going to be two commands that he would repeat throughout the scan. Hold and breathe. Once he uttered the first hold we were underway.

Back to those earplugs I talked of earlier. When the machine got going I had never been so happy to have my ears stuffed with little pieces of foam. For everyone that's had a scan, that unmistakable sound is something you'll never forget. BAA BAA BAA BAA, ba ba ba ba ba ba ba ba. This annoying pattern of slow piercing noise followed by quick rapid fire of the same nuisance repeated itself for the next hour and change. However, I don't think they knew who they were dealing with. Within ten minutes of receiving my first hold/breathe commands and tolerating that crazy noise I was knocked out.

Being able to sleep anywhere and under any circumstance paid great dividends each and every time I needed a scan. On that day however, Score? Me: 1 Machine: 0. Before I knew it I was being removed from the tunnel and it was over. As the bed I was laying on gradually exited, light began to pierce my senses and I heard a voice asking how I was doing. How was I doing? I was just interrupted from one of the greatest naps ever. How did they think I was doing? Naturally, I asked if I could lay there for a few more minutes. Baffled they obliged.

Somehow that confined space had become extremely comfortable. A few moments later I sat up and the technician asked how long I had been sleeping. In typical form I asked how long I had been in there. About seventy five minutes you say?

Yup, that's about right, I replied.

You slept the entire time?

The technician stood there in amazement. Glad to see I hadn't lost my touch. Once I was dressed I rejoined my parents. Similar to the prior day when I had my sonogram, Dr. Katz would be taking a "wet" reading of the film as the test was ongoing. He would forward these initial results to both Dr. Goldberg and Dr. Brower whom I was about to meet.

First things first however, I was starving and food was a must. When we exited East River, there was a hot dog vendor on the corner. With eyes bigger than my stomach I would indulge in a hotdog with mustard, sauerkraut and onions and a knish. That may not be the right thing to have for your first meal, but it was heaven! With each bite my stomach thanked me. Now we could go meet Dr. Brower. Little did that vendor know, he would become my post scan ritual for the foreseeable future. We jumped in a taxi and we were on our way. We didn't have far to go, a little more than ten blocks to 61st and Lexington.

As we sat in the back seat of the taxi, my stomach began singing a new tune. Amongst my family my metabolism was a topic of astonishment and jokes as it was nothing for me to take a bite of a meal and have to excuse myself for the bathroom. However, this was something different. Someone had forgotten to tell us that all that iodine solution would act as a laxative and act it did. We couldn't get to Dr. Brower's office fast enough. No sooner than saying hello to Laura, the doctor's assistant, did I ask for the restroom. Now I couldn't tell you what it is about iodine that "activates" your system but boy oh boy it was something. By the time I actually met Dr. Brower I must have lost five pounds. I know this is a lot of information, but what's a bowel movement amongst friends? Pretty sure my mom was mortified.

When I was finally finished, I met Nancy who would take samples of my blood. I had huge veins and needles never bothered me but she was talented. It was over before you knew it like nothing had happened. She was so good, that when someone else in the office tried to take my blood I would tell them I was superstitious and that only Nancy was allowed to do so. She took two samples, a CBC (Complete Blood Count) and a Chemistry. I had no clue why or what they meant but not only would I learn over time, I became adept at reading each report so that I could tell Dr. Brower and Laura my results. When the machine finished reading my blood Nancy gave me my printout to give to Laura. I rejoined my folks and a few moments later we met Dr. Brower.

Dr. Brower

He was a mild mannered man whose compassion showed immediately. We clicked instantly. At this point Dr. Brower had received both my blood workup and my initial CAT scan results. My parents and I sat in front of him as he began to speak. I wondered what went through his mind as he spoke. He sat there looking into the eyes of people he had never met before who were hanging onto his every word, knowing he was about to give them the worst news of their lives. Did that process weigh on him? How did he handle it? I knew at that moment we had no personal attachment other than a referral from his friend Dr. Goldberg but did he rehearse what he was about to say? Was he nervous? It's not every day that you meet someone and tell them they have cancer. Well, then again, maybe for him this was routine. After all, he was an oncologist and hematologist and this is what he did for a living.

In a soft spoken voice he began explaining that he had a chance to look at my results. At that point I checked out and began looking around his office. Who was this man? I scanned the numerous diplomas on the wall. Impressed with his accolades and the universities from which they came I changed my focus to the pictures on and around his desk. He was a family man with two sons. His sons were a bit younger than me but he was a father. Hmmm, We're in the right place. We're in good hands, I thought to myself. Not that I knew what I was looking for or talking to myself about, but it worked for me. Somehow that bit of information I had gathered in observation made a difference. I returned my attention to the matter at hand and listened to what he was saying.

So I've had a chance to review Danny's films from this morning and I'm terribly sorry to have to be the one to tell you this but he definitely has cancer.

With that my mom loses it again. Lately, it seemed like this had been happening a great deal. My dad, although emotional did his absolute best to be strong and the rock of the family. As for me, I was sitting there as indifferent as could be. All I knew was I still had this cold that was kicking my butt. Dr. Brower on the other hand had clearly traveled this road before and he understood both the gravity and emotion of the moment. He reached out and offered my mom a tissue. Despite being equipped with tissues nothing had prepared her for this moment, she accepted his offer.

Dr. Brower was poised. I marveled at his sustained calm. He allowed my parents to gather themselves before he continued so that they would be able to process the information. As my parents wiped their tears and took a few deep breaths they were able to regain some composure. I noticed my dad's leg rocking up and down and my mom was holding his hand. Today they happened to sit next to each other and I sat on my dad's right. It's almost as if they anticipated the news and planned our seating strategically so they would have each other's support immediately accessible.

Dr. Brower continued. "I apologize for the news but let me tell you what we do know at this time. Whatever form of cancer Danny has is pretty advanced. I would say he's had it for anywhere from a year and a half to two years."

WHAT???!!! My mom blurted out and stopped Dr. Brower dead in his tracks.

A year and a half to two years!!!
How is this possible?
I don't understand.

That doesn't make any sense.

I know it's difficult to understand but it's true.

His cancer ranges from his neck to his pelvic area.

But that's his entire torso!

Are you sure?

At this point I think my mom was about to pass out! If my folks hadn't arranged the seating the way they had I think she would have fallen out of her chair as my dad was practically holding her up.

I am sure, Dr. Brower replied.

Based upon the size of his organs and the area in which his cancer has spread, that paints a picture that tells us a great deal.

The entire time this conversation is going on I'm sitting there as if they're talking randomly about someone else, almost as if I wasn't there at all. Recognizing that I had been left out of the exchange, Dr. Brower turned his attention to me. As a parent, I know he understood why the focus thus far had been on my folks.

Danny, do you understand what I've been saying?

Do you have any questions?

I was as carefree as ever.

Nope, no questions.

Actually, I do have one.

What do we do now?

Good question.

There is one test that I would like to perform today if that's alright with you.

Sure, I have no plans.

Dr. Brower and my folks actually chuckled. Somehow the mood in the room had lightened just slightly. I wasn't trying to be funny, but I truly didn't have any other plans. In addition to prescribing medicine to combat the fever I had been battling, Dr. Brower went on to explain that he wanted to give me a physical and perform a bone marrow test. We all knew what a physical was but neither my folks nor I had ever heard of the latter. A bone marrow test is quite intricate. He explained that it involved a cork screw like mechanism that literally has to be screwed into your hip to extract bone marrow. Sounds great doesn't it?

The purpose of the test is to determine the category of cancer that

I had (i.e. lymphoma, leukemia etc.) and potentially how severe it was. It sounded simple enough to me. Of course my folks, especially my mom had additional questions but I guess that's what parents are for. At the end of all the questioning, Dr. Brower made it clear that we should all hope for Hodgkin's Disease which was a form of lymphoma. Often called the young person's disease because a good number of young people get it, it has become one of the most successful forms of cancer to treat. If it weren't Hodgkin's my prognosis wouldn't be the greatest due to the advanced nature of what we were dealing with. With all that said and understood, Dr. Brower showed me to his examination room and my parents returned to the reception area.

Prior to starting the bone marrow test he performed a thorough examination and recorded my weight. At the time I was nearly six feet tall and weighed in at a thoroughly skinny 140 pounds. Back then I preferred to call myself thin as if that added on a few pounds but make no mistake, I was skinny. My weight which got logged at the beginning of every visit would become a key indicator in the months to come. He checked all of my glands which despite knowing I had them all over, I learned at that moment they are literally everywhere. The two areas in which he focused were my groin and underarms. At one point he lifted my arm and proceeded to put his hand deep into my arm pit. Before I knew it, it felt like he was playing my ribs like guitar strings. Not only did this feel weird, in the following days it would grow sore. Eventually, both my arm pits and I got used to this prodding. After we finished a round of questions regarding how I had been feeling we began to talk about the bone marrow test.

Bone Marrow Test

Now Danny, prior to the actual test I have to administer a set of three needles each with its own purpose. The first we'll use to numb the area around your hip. The second will be used to go a bit further and numb your inner layers of tissue. With each of the first two needles you'll feel a good pinch. The third needle however will go straight into your nerve. Unfortunately, there's nothing I can do about numbing you for this one as it will hurt. However, it is the most important. After the medicine takes hold and you're numb we'll begin. Essentially from that point on you'll feel pressure, but no pain.

I understood everything Dr. Brower had said. It didn't sound like fun but this was the party I had been invited to so I figured it was time to dance. Dr. Brower began to prep his instruments. Out came the first three needles. As I mentioned I've never had a problem with needles but these sonsabitches were no ordinary needles. Each one was longer than the next. Practically urban legends in their own right, they were unlike anything I had ever seen before. The third needled immediately embedded an image in my brain that lasts to this day. Although probably not as long as I recall, from end to end I remember it being nearly a foot long. The fourth and final needle indeed resembled a cork screw. The needle itself was the thickest thing ever. The opening where the marrow would get sucked into was about the same size of the opening of a ball point pen. It was a bit ominous to think that had to be screwed into my hip. Then he laid out a number of rectangular microscope slides.

Assuming screwing this thing into my hip meant it was going into my side, I laid down on the examination table on my back only to learn that I was mistaken. Apparently the side of your hip has way too many nerves to attempt such a procedure. Instead we would use the area of the hip close to the small of my back so I would be required to lie on my side. Despite knowing the shape of hip bones, I actually thought my hips were only on my side but learned differently that day. My journey had only just started but I was getting one heck of an education. Once Dr. Brower cleaned the area we were ready. He was extremely good about explaining each step as it happened.

Ok, here goes the first needle. You're going to feel a slight pinch.
And pinch it did.
Alright, that one is finished.

A couple minutes later after the first few layers of skin and tissue were numb we were ready for the second needle.

Okay, one more time, slight pinch.

The second needle was a bit different. Initially there was pressure as if something was happening but I didn't really feel it. Then in an instant the pinch arrived. It left nearly as fast. We paused a few more moments to let it take effect. We were now ready for the urban legend. This mamba jamba was the king of his peers and towered above all others. I should have known something was up because right before giving me the third needle, Dr. Brower apologized. Take my word for it, if you ever go to the doctor and they apologize prior to doing something, that shit is gonna HURT!!!

He instructed me to hold onto the table and brace myself. Quite often in life the warning/buildup to an event is greater than the event itself. Trust me when I tell you, in this instance, that wasn't the case. Similar to the second needle I felt pressure again as it started but that's where all comparisons ended. All of a sudden it was like someone lit a match inside of me and dowsed it with gasoline causing an explosion. WOW!!! **WOW!!!** Despite being instructed to remain as still as possible while the needle was inside me, I'm certain my entire body jolted and I nearly flew off the table. Sweat began to pour off my brow, I was breathing intensely and my eyes surely bulged out of their sockets. There was no comparing this to any other feeling as it was in a class of its own. Dr. Brower immediately apologized.

Sorry about that.

Yeah me too!!!

At least I hadn't lost my sense of humor. A few minutes later I couldn't feel a thing and we were ready for the main attraction. With one hand holding onto my side he began screwing that cork screw like needle into my hip. The only thing I felt was intense pressure but no pain. Eerily though, I could hear the cork screw grinding its way crunch after crunch towards its destination. Ordinarily having incredibly strong bones is a good thing. Unfortunately however, this did not work in my doctor's favor as it created an exceptionally difficult amount of work for him. Honestly, as the test progressed I actually began feeling really bad for him. Having spoke with a friend whose mom recently had a bone marrow test I learned that the technology has not changed for this procedure but somehow it seems like there has to be a better way.

Having expected the entire procedure to take between 20 and 30 minutes, the 30 minute mark came and went with nothing to show for his efforts. Proving to be more challenging than anticipated, Dr. Brower was forced to take a brief time out to wipe his brow and get a sip of water. The cork screw remained embedded in my hip. At this point he was sweating as if he had gone to the gym. Technically I guess he had. He explained that things were going to take longer than expected as I had the strongest bones he had ever encountered. After his brief break we started again. Even though he was doing all the work we were in this together. I felt like cheering him on but figured that might be a bit strange. After all, how would that have sounded? "C'mon Dr. Brower, you can do it." "Yeah, thanks kid."

About fifteen minutes later Dr. Brower let me know he had finally reached the marrow. Seconds later I heard the most depressed sounding: "Oh no." I might have been nonchalant, but as a matter of reference, any time you're doctor is performing a procedure on you and he or she says "Oh no," it's definitely not good. Being as though I was facing the opposite direction I had no idea what was wrong.

I hate to tell you this, but we're going to have to start all over again.
You're bones are so strong they broke the needle.

Right then he showed me what had started out 45 minutes earlier as a straight instrument, came out of me shaped like an L. More than a bit depressed at the thought of having to repeat this whole process he looked exhausted. Not that I was indifferent at this point but what choice did I have? We were already there, might as well finish. Dr. Brower retrieved a new cork screw and let me know it shouldn't take as long this time around. Fortunately for both of us, fifteen minutes later he was able to retrieve all the bone marrow he needed. When we were finished, he asked me if I wanted to see what all the fuss was about. Funny looking stuff that bone marrow. It was kind of yellow like with a pink tint from blood. Not sure what I had expected but somehow it seemed like he had gotten short changed for all his work.

The wound was pretty nondescript and would heal on its own

without stitches. I just couldn't shower that evening and had to change the bandage twice a day starting the following morning. Then in my eyes he gave me probably the worst news I had received yet.

Now unfortunately, even if you have the energy, you can't play any sports whatsoever right now.

WHAT???

Was he kidding? Can't play sports? Was this a cruel joke? I couldn't wait to feel better and go outside to join my friends. How about that for priorities? Not much more than an hour ago I had been told I definitely had cancer and all I could think about was going outside to play. Refusing to believe that I was basically getting grounded I had to know more.

Dr. Brower went on to explain that with my spleen being nearly two and a half to three footballs in size, apparently I was in jeopardy of having it explode. That was great and all, but I had been playing sports all year prior to getting diagnosed and nothing had happened so why all the fuss now? In general, an enlarged spleen can be in jeopardy of rupturing if the abdominal cavity sustains a blow. This was especially true in my case as my spleen was about twenty times the normal size. With it so swollen Dr. Brower told me that even if I simply decided to go for a stroll I had to have someone walk in front of me to make sure I didn't get bumped as even that could cause my spleen to burst. Combine that with the fact that I played hockey, sports instantly became off limits. Almost as if to see if playing sports really wasn't an option, I pressed further.

Really?

Die?

How long would it take?

Would I know if it burst?

Even though we had only met that morning, Dr. Brower began to realize how hard headed I was so he stated it a little more clearly.

Let me put it this way, if it does burst I wouldn't stop for pizza on the way to the hospital if I were you. You'd only have ten to fifteen minutes before your blood stream becomes completely poisoned and if that happens, as I said you can die.

Well, since it was put that way he had made his point and I agreed to lay low. Happy that he did, he now invited me to rejoin my parents. I always wondered if he had exaggerated slightly to combat my stubbornness.

He walked me to the waiting room where my parents eagerly awaited my return. The four of us reconvened in Dr. Brower's office where he reviewed my bone marrow test and told us that we should have the results within a couple of days at the latest. He went on to tell my parents the same news he had just given me that by no means should I play any sports. Damn doc, not that I didn't plan on listening, but now that my folks knew I definitely had no chance! All this talk of what I wasn't allowed got me thinking. As soon as we had finished talking with Dr. Brower I asked to speak with him in private for a moment.

Uhm, doc I have a quick question.

So I know I'm not allowed to play sports but uhm…am I allowed to have sex?

C'mon, that's a natural question for anyone and I was seventeen with raging hormones. If I wasn't going to be allowed to play sports I had to have some form of recreation. I hung onto his words as if my life depended on it. I know I know, my priorities were a bit skewed but I couldn't help it. Fortunately Dr. Brower gave me the green light with one exception.

You can have sex, but just don't try to be Superman.

Take it easy!

WooHOO! I could definitely live with that. I left Dr. Brower's office and rejoined my parents. As soon as we were in the elevator my dad said, "You asked him if you could have sex didn't you?" Guess he knew me real well. We all shared a laugh on the way down.

The Waiting

The next couple of days while we waited for my bone marrow test results were a bit anxious. Even though the outcome of my test was expected to take two days, it was possible they could have come as early as the following day. This definitely didn't help my parent's nerves as they seemed to be going crazy. My poor mom practically jumped out of her seat to answer the phone every time it rang. Over and over again she would rip the phone off the hook before it would even finish ringing once.

Hello???!!!

Each time she answered, whoever was on the other end could sense something was up as she'd usually follow her greeting with "No, I'm just waiting for Danny's results." She would always keep her conversations brief so she wouldn't tie up the phone as this was the 90s and we didn't have call waiting. Two days after my test, the call she had so eagerly been awaiting arrived. Like clockwork she jumped at the phone.

Hello???!!!

This time there was no explanation to the person on the other end as to why she answered so quickly. Instead there was a moment of silence. I knew from the sound or lack thereof that this was the one. I was in the living room and my mom was in the kitchen, but there was an unmistakable muffled orchestra of sorrow that cast its medley from afar. A mixture of crying, silence and "I see's" repeated over and over as if they were a record that was skipping. With one brief "Okay, thank you" the conversation was over.

The receiver found its way back to the cradle and with it that medley of sorrow found its return as well. My mom was having a moment. It was her moment and I knew she needed to have it all to herself. I had been sleeping on the couch, so when I heard my mom peek out to see if I was awake I made sure to lie still as if I hadn't heard the phone ring. She quickly walked passed the living room on the way to her bedroom where she closed the door to be alone. Despite living in a prewar building with thick walls there was no amount of concrete that could mute the sound coming from her room that day.

She was mad, angry, hurt and helpless all at once. It was a pain I've never heard before or since. That initial shock and disbelief was unlike anything else. I could hear an unmistakable pounding of her fist on the bed accompanied by "Why, why, why" mixed in with the blowing of her nose and coughing. She was sobbing. She couldn't breathe. She was practically choking. I've heard it said that a mother's love is unparalleled and the raw emotion piercing through the walls that afternoon was a testament to that fact. From the day I was born, I had been trouble to put it kindly.

She nearly died at my birth. Beginning in nursery school I had pneumonia several years in a row with extremely high fevers. She had been through the ringer with me and yet somehow the worst of it still awaited us. I could tell from the sound in her room that she would have done anything she could have to protect me and trading places would have been her pleasure. That was the type of mom she was and is.

As her cries continued I couldn't help but want to make everything better. I was so sorry for her pain as I hadn't gotten sick on purpose. I didn't know how to change our circumstances. Actually, I didn't even know what our circumstances were. Make no mistake though, they were *our* circumstances. We were in this together. I knew that and if felt great. At some point I heard my mom pick up the phone. Once again she had the arduous task of calling my dad. I can't imagine the courage it took to make such a call but she found it. I know I said it before, but I marvel at her strength.

I heard her say hello. The sound of my dad's voice must have sent her emotions spiraling as her following words were barely audible. Knowing that we were awaiting "The news," what were my dad's thoughts when he heard my mom crying? How did he react? Words weren't needed as her reaction told the story. Her emotion intensified as the nose blowing, coughing and choking returned. Despite being on the phone it seemed, my parents were having a moment together. For a few minutes, there were no words coming from the other side of the wall. Then a few "I knows" and "Okays" began to surface. I could only think that my dad was doing his best to comfort, be strong and reassure my mom that everything would work out. After a couple more "Okays" the phone once again found its way back to the cradle. It was quite some time before my mom came out of her room.

In the interim my thoughts turned to the other side of that phone. Undoubtedly my dad had just been strong for both of them but who was going to be strong for him? I'm sure he was in his office at the restaurant when he received my mom's call. As they both hung up what was the scene? I have no doubt that anything within reach was in jeopardy of taking flight. My dad was a rock but his children and family were a soft spot. What was he going through?

No matter how strong he had just been for my mom I know that was how weak he was feeling on the inside the instant he hung up the phone. That kryptonite that found him days earlier in Dr. Goldberg's office was beaming with force and right then he surely surrendered before it. He had always told me there is nothing worse than a parent losing a child and I know being smacked with that mere thought process and possibility was too much. We're more than father/son, we're best friends. I closed my eyes as if somehow he could hear my thoughts.

It's ok pop, we'll be ok!

Promise!

When my mom finally emerged she had completely gathered herself and for the most part was her usual cheery self. We shared general conversation and pleasantries but it wasn't until my dad returned home that evening that we discussed Dr. Brower's phone call together. On each parallel wall of the living room, we had two couches that faced one another and the two of them were sitting on one while I lay on the other as we all watched television. On a commercial break my dad turned off the T.V. and said we had to talk.

Having been aware of the events from earlier that day I was as prepared as I could be. Both of them were very calm and matter a fact as if they had rehearsed their words. They did their absolute best to stay strong for their baby as they told me I had an advanced stage of lymphoma, but we still needed to know exactly what type of cancer I had. Therefore, the following morning we would be meeting with Dr. Clarke, a surgeon who would perform a biopsy which would determine exactly that. My mom had a tissue in her hand and she wiped her eyes as they delivered "the news."

Surgeon?

Biopsy?

I sat there bewildered. These were unknown facts that my

eavesdropping had not produced. Either way, this was all new to me and in my eyes seemingly part of an adventure. Would I be able to "choose" my own path and outcome as in the series of novels my sister had given me years earlier? After all, those always seemed to turn out well. What did I need a biopsy for? Hadn't I just had a bone marrow test? Apparently both have their own purpose. The first is a wider scope and tells you the general category of cancer while the latter narrows it down to the specific type. There was no option of choice here. My path was set in stone. Bright and early the next day we met Dr. Clarke.

He was a tall man, about 6'5". With broad shoulders and big hands, in my eyes his stature resembled that of an athlete more than it did a surgeon. Certainly at one point in time he had played power forward or tight end. There we were on the verge of a different game of sorts and I intended to know if he was as competent as his appearance. As if I knew what to look for I paid particular attention to the details I had always been taught to be important. Strong handshake: check. Eye contact: check. Batting two for two there was only one more thing to look for. As he spoke I stared intently at his hands. If they shook or trembled I was out of there! Nope, three for three.

He had passed my little mock test and that was good enough for me. When did we get started? If it were convenient we could start right then. The entire procedure was going to be pretty straightforward. He was going to make a slight cut at the base of my neck near my collarbone about two inches long. The whole thing was scheduled to take no more than an hour and a half. There would be minimal scarring. Scarring? Cool! They added character right? Either way, this was a pretty standard procedure. Despite having a form of local anesthesia that rendered me silly, I was going to be an out-patient and best of all I didn't need to fast. Did I say that I didn't need to fast? This guy was the greatest. Let's get started.

Pump your breaks young fella. My mom had brought a list of questions with her. C'mon Ma! What else did we need to know? He had already passed my test. She proceeded to ask an array of questions that left me dizzy. I didn't even know what she was talking about. Time and length of procedure, how many stitches, how much pain to expect, recuperation time and apparently the most important; when would we get the results? The room was spinning. Who asks so many questions?

It was clear this whole process was more serious to my folks as I still didn't fully comprehend what was happening. All the answers were listened to intently but the one regarding the timing of the results drew quite interesting attention from my folks. I hadn't realized that the waiting to find out what we had learned thus far had weighed on them tremendously. Apparently it wasn't necessarily the results they feared most, not knowing the outcome and stressing about the "what if," drove them equally insane.

Evidently we were not allowed to leave Dr. Clarke's office until my mom was satisfied with all the answers she received. It wasn't that I didn't have questions of my own, they were just simpler. "Would I be allowed to go out and hang with my friends when it was finished?" Now that's priorities, I tell you. As I said, once my mom was satisfied with all the answers we were good. Everyone stood up, shook hands and said good day. We were scheduled to reconvene the following morning at 8 a.m. at New York Hospital.

We were up early the following morning and my folks seemed to be on edge. Instead of going to the hospital it felt like we were getting ready to go to the airport for a flight. My mom was super organized. She made all of our timing clear. With an 8 a.m. check in we should be up by six and out of the house by seven in case there was traffic. When I got up they were in the kitchen having their coffee and my mom had already showered. What time had they gotten up? Had they slept? This seemed to be a pattern as of late. All I knew when I woke was that I was allowed to eat breakfast and that if I felt well enough I was allowed to hang out with my friends afterwards. Dr. Clarke was the greatest.

We arrived at the hospital early. My sister who was away at college in Wisconsin, had been continuously filled in with all appropriate details by my mom. She actually wanted to come home to be with me because she felt I could tell her the things I wouldn't reveal to my parents. Even though that was probably true my folks didn't want her to leave school. We didn't use email and cell phones yet, so she would actually have to be in her house or call home for each update.

Biopsy

Shortly after we finished all of our hospital paper work a nurse came to get me. I gave my parents a hug and a kiss and I was off. Their mood was nervous but they were holding up. From there my nurse took me to a separate area of the hospital. Now athletics are my first true love and it was then I came to the realization that having surgery was quite similar to preparing for a big game. In sports you have your pre game routines that include getting taped, dressed and warmed up which is truly not much different from some of the pre-op customs. After all, you have to change into that lovely green robe and put on your footsies with the cool grips on the bottom. Game time is the operation itself and post-op is post game where you recuperate.

Now once you're ready for surgery you wait in a room comparable to a locker room until someone comes to get you.

Hi Daniel, are you ready?

Do I have a fucking choice?

Cause' I don't know about you but I could think of several things I'd rather be doing.

Naturally, I didn't say those things, but with my smart mouth I couldn't help but think of a couple off the cuff remarks. Anyway, once I agreed, we were on our way. I started walking down a cold dimly lit hallway on the way to the Big Show. It's the calm before the storm. Off in the distance you can see bright lights peeking through windows of a door. The only thing missing is the roar of a crowd. If this isn't similar to walking down the tunnel on the way to a game or a boxing match I don't know what is. All I needed was for someone to cue "Eye of the Tiger" and it would have been perfect.

Upon arrival in the operating room, I really was under the bright lights. This might be the coldest brightest room I've ever been in. There's a bunch of people doing...well I don't really know what they were doing but I assumed they were doing it well. You're shown to the operating table which is equally as cold if not colder than the room itself. Oh and I mean cold. So cold in fact I could hear George from "Seinfeld" shaking his hands screaming "I was in the pool! I was in the pool!!!"

While you're lying down you're brought a blanket so you don't freeze to death. Then someone starts an IV and cleans the area of "interest." After that Dr. Clarke came over and started schmoozing.

So, how's it going?

Feeling alright today?

Yeah sure...Besides the fact that you're about to cut open my neck, I'm feeling great!

He chuckled and continued to outline the area with a marker and did his best to make me feel at ease. Then the anesthesiologist made an appearance. They talked for a few minutes and let me know what they were about to give me as if I would recognize those words I had never heard before. Despite not having a choice, it was very democratic like. They're so polite they even asked if I was ready. Was this a trick question? Once I said yes, they got started and injected the anesthesia.

Alright Danny, I want you to count backwards from ten.

Clearly a request I could oblige.

Sure.

Ten.

Nine.

Eight.

And that was it. That was all I remember saying before knocking out. Whatever they injected, knocked me out silly. This has to be the best moment of entertainment everyone in the OR waits for. Honestly I could see everyone placing bets on how fast it knocks someone out. Imagine the scene. Doctors, technicians, nurses etc hollering "I got $20 on eight. I got $20 on nine." No more bets. No more bets. It's one big game of roulette.

At some point I remember waking slightly during the procedure.

Hey, I can feel that!

I think I need some more of that good stuff.

Feel What? Dr Clarke replied.

That right there.

You just cut me.

It was funny, in addition to "feeling" something, I could actually hear it as well. It sounded like a muted version of a piece of paper being torn. Dr. Clarke couldn't believe it.

You felt that?

Yeah.

In an instant the anesthesiologist gave me some more of that good stuff and immediately I was "nice" again and didn't feel or hear a thing. Before I knew it, Dr. Clarke was waking me back up and helping me off the table. I don't remember getting from the OR to post-op but somehow I got there. When I awoke, I heard that infamous beep beep beep and in what it seemed to take a few minutes, I opened my eyes to be greeted by spotlights glaring directly on me.

Truly, the placement of the lights which seem to be perfectly in your line of vision are blinding. Isn't there something that can be done about this? Why should anyone's first glimpse back into the world, be accompanied by the thought "I can't see." Comforting however, is the fact that once you do fully open your eyes and get adjusted to the brightness, someone is there to greet you.

Hello Daniel, how are you feeling?

Where had they come from? Was there a sensor on my eyelids that let them know I was waking up? Before I knew it my mom and dad were there as well. Shit, who knew? It's a party. What's next? A Carvel ice cream cake with the crunchies would have been nice!

Shortly after I was reunited with my parents, Dr. Clarke came to check on me. He had already spoken with my folks but he wanted to tell me all had gone well and that I did a good job. Naturally of course! Then he stunned me with his next comment.

You're quite the talker eh?

Huh?

I remembered waking up for that quick minute when I needed more of the good stuff but what was he talking about? He went on to inform me and my folks that I actually talked throughout the entire procedure. Was he kidding? He was not. In fact, he told me about the sports I played, my family and even my nasty English teacher I had despised so. I was dumbfounded! Here I thought we had a brief five minutes of interaction when in fact it was more like 90. Guess I was right, that was some "good stuff."

While I was in recuperation, they brought me some apple juice and a couple of cookies. Oh now it's okay for me to have apple juice? I wish someone would have gotten that memo a couple days prior when I was having my CAT scan. Anyway, shortly after finishing my snack I was cleared to go. My neck was quite stiff and the stitches and tape they had put over the incision were pulling my head towards my right side. I felt a little bit awkward, but it was a beautiful late fall day and all I could think about was hanging out with my friends. After all, Dr. Clarke had said if I felt alright I could do so.

My parents were true sports and they drove me down Second Avenue to Stuyvesant High School or at least where Stuy used to be on 15th street so that I could hang out with my friends for a spell. I actually went to Forest Hills High School in Queens, but the majority of my friends went to Stuy and that's where I spent the bulk of my time. The old Stuy was so lackadaisical I had even attended class there on occasion. There was a small park down the block from the school where everyone would hang out during lunch or simply if they didn't want to go to class. It didn't matter what time of day it was, there were always a handful of kids in that park. When we showed up it was around lunch time so the place was packed. At seventeen, a bandage across your neck was a badge of honor. It could not have been cooler and all my friends marveled over it. Sheesh, if I knew that was the reaction it was going to get, we could do this on a weekly basis. It was a beautiful sunny day and truth be told I didn't have a care in the world. After hanging out with my friends briefly my parents and I went downtown and got knishes from Yonah Schimmel's. It was the simple things that made me happy and continue to do so.

For me the next couple of weeks were truly a breeze. In the

morning hours technically I had school. The Board of Education may be regarded as slow acting but to their credit, as soon as it was determined I was unable to physically attend school they provided me with a teacher that came to my house so that I wouldn't fall behind. My mom had to go to school to speak with the principal and fill out paperwork, but once that was done we received a call from my new teacher, Professor Stoddard, and he arrived within a matter of days. He was a great guy and totally understood that at times I was extremely low on energy so we worked around my ebbs and flows. Professor Stoddard enabled me to keep pace and ensured that I graduated on time. Instead of following a mundane routine, he let me study subjects we didn't cover in school like law. We applied our learning to real life situations and subjects that previously gave me difficulty instantly started clicking. Selfishly, quite possibly the best thing about him was the grade he gave me in English.

Prior to him being assigned to me, my lovely English teacher back at school had given me a 55 due to excessive absences despite the fact that everyone at school had been informed of my situation and all my other teachers had written absences due to illness on my report card. Somehow for her, it appeared this was personal. However, after working with me for a few weeks Professor Stoddard knew I wasn't a 55 student and fortunately for me, he had the ultimate say over my final grades and I received an 85 in English which technically came from my "favorite" teacher back at school. I bet she choked when she saw the grade she had essentially given me. So as far as I was concerned, being sick had at least one benefit.

More Waiting

Back at the ranch however, my folks did their best to keep their minds occupied while we waited endlessly for my biopsy results. Despite being told it would take a couple of weeks to receive them, knowing that and actually hanging around day by day trying to do anything to pass the time was entirely different. The forewarning did nothing to calm their anxiety. My mom once again seemed to launch herself out of her chair like a rocket every time the phone dared to ring. "HELLO?" she exulted before a second ring could sound off. Each time she answered and someone other than Dr. Brower had the nerve to be on the other end she'd follow what was anxiousness disguised as excitement with "No, we're just waiting for the doctor to call with Danny's results." Was this déjà vu? It surely seemed like we had been here before. Was this to be the ritual every time we awaited an outcome of a test? This seemed a little crazy to me, but my folks explained this was something I couldn't possibly comprehend. Apparently, this was one of those things I'd understand when I became a parent myself. Much to my mom's chagrin this is an event she's still waiting for but that's another story for another day.

As you're aware, when that phone call finally came I was sleeping in my preferred spot on the couch. This time I never heard the phone ring. Instead I only heard the aftermath that led to one of the purest moments that my mother and I have ever shared. We hugged and cried and at some point my mom retreated back to her bedroom. Although permanently etched in my reality, when the dust settled, that moment evaporated as quickly as it had arrived. It was then my mom had to muster up the strength to once again call my dad and sister to deliver the news. How many of these calls was she forced to make?

Now that our results were in, the next morning it was time for another trip to Dr. Brower's office to discuss strategy. This was so official like. Strategy? Were we going to battle? As we sat in his office and the discussion began it was clear to me this day was different. Despite the nervousness my parents carried, there was a sense of calm in the room that day. The suspense had been lifted and I believe that fact that we knew our nemesis put my folks slightly at ease. They could now point their energy in a direction and found comfort in that fact.

Game Plan

As Dr. Brower spoke he laid out a time frame for my treatment, what stage of cancer I had and what kind of chemotherapy I was going to get. There are four stages of Hodgkin's and mine was between the third and fourth stage. Had my cancer been Non-Hodgkin's lymphoma, that would have decreased my odds to 50-50 at best. Instead we started off with a 90% chance of making it. I was scheduled to undergo eight cycles each a month long, however, it actually took closer to nine months in total. Each cycle consisted of two weeks of injections in conjunction with three weeks of pills followed by one week off in order to let my body recoup from the destruction accompanied by those five letters. Chemo. With that said, to combat my cancer we were going to use MOPP ABVD without the D.

Funny, I've never even cared what most of those letters stood for and with the exception of two of them, I don't have a clue what they mean to this day. All I know is that they brought the ruckus. Dr. Brower explained that despite being designed to rid my body of cancer, it wouldn't focus solely on the bad and unfortunately would destroy the good as well. What did all this mean? Well, prior to starting chemo however, apparently I had to make several visits to a sperm bank. A sperm bank? Yup! There was a 50-50 chance that post chemo, my little tad poles wouldn't have the same swimming capacity as they once did. Therefore, if I wanted to ensure that I had a batch of healthy tad poles, I had to make a few "donations."

Going to a sperm bank… I'm not sure how many of you have ever had the pleasure but believe me it's not an experience I recommend. Especially at seventeen when you have to be accompanied by a parent, it can be quite awkward. Of course in this case my dad went with me. Oh yeah, did I mention that I had never masturbated before? I know this sounds crazy and you might be thinking how is that possible? Well, I was seventeen with a girlfriend that took care of all those things.

Prior to making my donation, we had to call them to confirm

my first appointment. How many appointments were there going to be? What did I have to do? Well, that part was actually pretty self-explanatory. I was on one phone in my room while my dad listened on the other receiver in the living room.

Hi this is Danny Alotta.

I'm a patient of Dr. Brower's and I'm calling to confirm my appointment for tomorrow at noon.

So far this seemed easy enough as Laura, Dr. Brower's assistant had made the appointment. The person who answered the phone at the "bank" had me in their book as scheduled so we were good to go. However, this was all new to me.

Excuse me, I do have a couple of questions.

Do you know how many times I have to donate?

I don't know about you but this seemed like a normal question under the circumstances. Unfortunately the response from the other end of the phone was anything but.

You can come here as many times as you'd like.

Huh? Are you kidding me? Was this a joke? A play on words perhaps? Come here as many times as you like? Was she trying to be funny? I was pissed.

What do you mean as many times as I'd like?

I don't want to come there, I don't have a choice.

I didn't make this appointment, my doctor did!

Common sense would make you think my response might elicit some compassion. After all, I'm sure Laura had told them how old I was and I'm even more positive they were familiar with Dr. Brower as he probably sent them patients regularly. Clearly the woman on the other ends next response elicited stupidity as opposed to compassion or simply common sense.

Why, what's wrong with you?

At this point they should have changed their name to I don't have a clue because I couldn't believe this. I was heating up!!!

What do you mean what's wrong with me?

What's wrong with you?

Don't you have any of my information?

My dad couldn't take it anymore. If you know my dad, there's no explanation needed. He's old school Sicilian. Oh he's Italian you say? No, he's Sicilian and there's a difference. Just as the food in Sicily is spicier than its mainland counterpart so are the tempers. A mere conversation in Sicily carries with it a level of passion that from the outside looking in could appear like an argument. Witnessing an argument itself...Fahgettaboutit! My dad is a ball of fire especially when it comes to protecting his children and the nincompoop on the other end of the phone had just crossed the imaginary line in the sand.

HEY!!!

This is Danny's father and I'm going to need you to be aware of the situation.

He begins chemotherapy soon and that's why he's coming in.

Why else do you think his ONCOLOGIST made the appointment?

Huh?

For shits and giggles?

I know I nearly choked so the person on the other end was surely a gasp.

Oh, I'm so sorry.

I didn't have the information in front of me.

I... I...

I don't care what your reasoning is.

Anyway, Danny go ahead...

Immediately I had the attention of the person on the other end. Now remember, at this point in my life I had never masturbated before so naturally I wanted to know if I could bring my girlfriend with me. True to form, the genius on the other end had no clue so she put us on hold to find out. While we were waiting my dad and I had our own conversation.

Pop does she know anything?

She can't answer any of my questions.

It's not like I'm doing this for the fun of it.

Much to our dismay, the voice on the other end returned. Clueless as ever they proceeded to tell us that no one knew the answer to my question. Are you fucking kidding me? In the history of this place I couldn't have been the first person to have asked if they could bring their girlfriend, wife, significant other, cat, dog, something, someone... How was this possible? It wasn't as if I was asking fifty questions.

Can you answer any of my questions?

All they could say was that they were sorry. Yeah, me too! With that I slammed the phone down.

Me and My Pop

This was the first time since my "process" had started that it hit me everything wasn't ok and that I was actually sick. I sat there on my bed in my room with the door closed. Taking deep breaths I tried to compose myself. It wasn't working. With that a tear struck my cheek. I was officially having my first emotional moment since this whole thing had started. Damn! How'd I get here? That initial tear had friends and they seemed to be on the verge of a party. Another tear fell followed by another and another. Sensing I wasn't in a good place, my dad had come to my room. I heard a knock at the door. Shit, there I was on the verge of uncontrollable emotion for the first time and my dad was at the door. I took a deep breath and wiped the tears from my face as fast as I could. However, if you know my dad, that knock at the door was simply a courtesy. He was coming in. He stood at the foot of my door with his hand on the door knob.

You ok?

Yeah, I just need a moment alone.

Sensing I was hurting he sat down next to me.

Letting me be alone wasn't an option for him. He was my protector and this was my weakest moment. He put his arm around me and I'll never forget what he said.

It's ok son. It's not your fault.

As he spoke, I was trying my best to be strong.

I know pop, I know.

Please, I just need to be alone for a minute.

With every word he held on tighter. He wasn't letting go. With that it was over. I had tried to be strong just like he had taught me but I couldn't take it anymore. Tears began to hit my lap at an uncontrollable pace. My breathing became sporadic. In between breaths I expressed my frustration and anger.

I mean she couldn't answer any of my questions.

This isn't my idea of fun.

I just don't understand!

What did I ever do to anyone?

I never hurt anybody!

I could no longer breathe. I was letting it all out. There I was practically choking yet my tears seemed to fall in slow motion. It was as if I could see each one drop individually. It was then that I noticed the flow of my tears hitting my lap seemed to double. In fact they had. I glanced to my right. My dad was crying with me at an even irrepressible pace. There we sat, father and son holding on to each other for dear life crying in one another's arms. I still had questions that needed answering.

Why did I get sick?

There are people that rob, steal; even murder and they live to be 100.

Where's the justice in that?

I never hurt anyone!

I just don't understand!!!

I know son, it's not fair!

Believe me it's not fair.

I wish I could trade places with you.

I'm so sorry! I love you so much!

I know pop. I love you too! I just don't understand.

I don't either, but the only thing we can do is fight this together. And that's how we're going to make it. TOGETHER! You'll see, we're going to be okay. I promise you son, we're going to be okay. I love you!

I know pop. I know. I love you too!

With that we began to attempt to catch our breath. My dad and I have had some amazing times together but that was perhaps the purest moment we ever spent. Interestingly, it wasn't until I wrote this that I realized my dad needed comfort that day as much as I did because truth be told, he was hurting worse me. He was my protector, powerful and in control. My being sick was out of his hands and seeing me hurt was a weight he couldn't bear.

The Sperm Bank

Despite the ineptness of the lady we spoke to, the following day my dad and I arrived as planned at noon. Although I'm sure there's more than one sperm bank in NYC and the fact that we would have liked to tell that lady to go to hell, time was of the essence and we stuck to the plan. Upon exiting the elevator and going through a large set of glass doors you enter a behemoth of a waiting room. Honestly, this place was huge. There was enough room to have a party there with at least 200 people. Did they know something that I didn't? Was this the most popular place in Manhattan and I just didn't know it? There weren't a lot of people sitting in the waiting room but they were certainly ready in case of a rush. Once checked in, like every other medical place I had been recently, you're handed a clipboard and told to fill out paperwork and answer some questions. I had envisioned the questioning here to have been a bit more interesting.

Come here often?

First time?

Was it as good for you as it was for me?

Instead it was the usual first name, last name, reason for coming, blah blah blah… Really? That's it? Of all the places, I would have at least expected a sperm bank to throw in a little humor with their questioning? Oh well. As usual, when you're finished, you bring your paperwork back to the receptionist. Here's where things begin to differ. At this point she comes from behind the counter with a few items in hand and tells you to follow her. I told my dad I'd see him in a little bit and shadowed the receptionist down a drab hallway. It was slightly past noon. She unlocked the third door on the right and showed me into one of the dingiest rooms I had ever seen. Then she handed me a crusty set of magazines and this little jar which she told me was for my specimen. My specimen? How scientific and professional. Where was all this professionalism the day before when I was asking my questions? Finally she gave me the key to the door and showed me how to lock it behind her.

At this point I began taking in my surroundings.

Beige walls.

Beige carpet.

Beige chair.

A small table.

A box of tissues.

My mind started spinning. *What on earth am I doing here? Look at this chair, it's crusty as hell. And these magazines… Are people shooting their load into the pages? Man, I don't want to touch anything in here. People come here for fun? They've got to be out of their minds!!! There has to be a way out. Damn, no window. Maybe I could sneak past reception, rejoin my dad and we could go get lunch? Yeah, probably not.*

Once reality hit, I realized there was no getting away. I placed my magazines and jar on the table next to the chair and closed my eyes as if by doing so I could escape my circumstance. Unfortunately, when I opened my eyes I remained in my crusty beige cubicle. With two fingers I grabbed the corner of a magazine and began to flip through the pages.

Are you kidding?

Oh yeah, this is gonna do it for me. Sure!

This is what I've always dreamt of. Looking through dirty magazines filled with "college girls" in a fuckin' sperm bank. I knew what I was talking about yesterday when I asked if I could bring my girlfriend. Shit, we could have been out of here by now. Oh well, might as well give this a try.

Now please remember, at this point in my life I had never masturbated. So I'm sitting there attempting to "handle" my situation. I literally took one tug at a time expecting something to happen. Of course it didn't so I took another, then another, and another. Again, nothing. Another tug. Nothing. This one tug ritual went on for such a long time that I wouldn't even have a clue as to how long. Void of any outcome other than this tug o war, I got so frustrated, I simply sat back and looked at my surroundings. Totally uninspired, I began to look at those college girls again.

Hey, there you are. Wink wink. *Just so you know, you're doing absolutely nothing for me but whatever.*

I began my one stroke at a time routine again which clearly went nowhere. I got so frustrated I literally started yelling at my member.

C'mon you stubborn fuck!

Do something already!

Do something!

C'mon!!!

Infuriated, I began taking it out on my friend. My one stroke routine got replaced by an attempt to beat him to hell. If he wasn't going to cooperate, at least he was going to feel my frustration. With that, all of a sudden things began to change.

Oh shit, I think this might be working.

Oh shit, it is working.

Damn, where's that cup?

There I sat in my crusty chair about to have an "epiphany" and now I had to find my cup to make a deposit. Doing all this while sitting down wasn't going to work so I stood up. There I was with my Johnson in one hand, trying to grab my cup with the other. "Ok, got it. Shit, it's a screw top! Are you kidding me? How the hell am I supposed to unscrew this damn thing and stay focused on the task at "hand" at the same time?" In quite possibly the most uncoordinated fashion I finally managed to get the top off my oversized Petri dish without skipping a beat. No sooner than I did, BOOM!!! The moment we had all been waiting for had finally arrived. With that, my sperm was shooting everywhere! The shit was hitting the wall, the ceiling, the carpet and like an idiot, there I was trying to catch it with that damn cup. How the hell was this supposed to work? Shouldn't this thing have come with some directions? By the time all was said and done, I eventually realized it was better to point my member into the cup. However, the wall, ceiling and carpet can attest that maybe 10% of my stuff made it into that cup. Hey, what did I know? I was a rookie. I had never been here or done this before.

Now that the fireworks had been set off, I had some cleaning up to do. I grabbed a couple of tissues, got myself together and exited my beige cave. Proud and feeling energized by what had just happened, I returned to the receptionist window to present my specimen. She held it up to the light, took one look at it and said "Uhm…you're going to need to make another appointment." When I finally returned to my dad in the waiting room I was greeted with astonishment.

What the hell were you doing in there?

You've been gone two and a half hours!!!

The clock read slightly after 2:30 in the afternoon. Innocently, I responded with "I told you I had never done that before!" My dad simply shook his head and we were off.

In the following week or so, I had to make a few more deposits. Each time you'll be glad to know I became more proficient at the task at hand. I came to find out that the nincompoop I had spoken with in advance of making my first deposit failed to tell me you're not supposed to have sex for a few days prior, which is something I had practically been doing before each visit. Hey, Dr. Brower said that I was allowed to. It probably resulted in me having to re-visit the bank more than I should have but at the end of the day what's a few extra tadpoles amongst friends?

Since no one knew whether or not I could bring my girlfriend with me to the sperm bank, I never did. She was my high school sweetheart. As with all first loves, we swore we were going to get married, have kids and a couple of dogs. That wasn't to be but to her credit, she stayed with me when I got sick and both myself and my parents appreciated that fact as she was able to provide a certain level of support only she was capable of doing. Obviously the time we spent together gradually diminished as not only didn't I have the energy to hang out regularly, it became unsafe for me to be around other people especially her since we were physically active. If she had a cold, kissing her could wind up killing me.

We talked a lot on the phone and she kept me as up to date as possible with the happenings at school. It wasn't the same as being there but at least it was something. Rarely did I discuss how I felt in general or about being sick as I didn't like to do so. It drove her crazy as she always wanted to know but I often talked to myself and tried to be a self healer. I think my process wore on her as when I required an additional operation she never came to visit me claiming she couldn't bear to see me like that. That's an interesting point as my being sick clearly wasn't just about me. It stopped the clock for everyone I was close to. For my girlfriend and I, what was supposed to be our glorious senior year together wound up being anything but. Understandably so, when all was said and done I'm not sure it was something she could handle as we broke up shortly after the operation I mentioned.

The weekend in between my visits to the sperm bank and actually starting chemotherapy, Dr. Brower had given my dad the okay to take me upstate for a couple of days as long as we promised that I got out of the car to walk around and stretch every 90 minutes or so since my spleen was dangerously large. That worked for me as I didn't mind the fresh air. My mom decided to stay home as I think she was extremely overwhelmed at that moment and needed time to gather herself.

It was going to be a father son weekend and off to Richfield Spring's we went to visit our close friends, the Schedivy's. Every time we visited them my dad brought cavatellis and meat sauce as that was tradition. The first night we always sparked the grill and had steaks, sausages and hot dogs. The Schedivy's were family and they knew everything that was going on. What they had yet to learn which my dad couldn't wait to tell Ray, the patriarch of the Shedivy clan was the episode from our recent experience at the sperm bank.

Once he brought it up I had no choice but to go into full detail. There I stood reenacting the entire situation from a few days earlier. In less time of course. The scene was comical. When everyone had learned that it took me two and a half hours to complete the task they were dumbfounded. When they learned that was my first time masturbating they nearly feel out of their chairs. Was I the only seventeen year old that had yet to masturbate? Regardless, watching me demonstrate my futile attempt to catch my sperm as it flew everywhere was one for the ages. That weekend provided the perfect amount of humor and relaxation. So much so, we almost forgot that a few days later I would begin chemo.

Before I officially started chemo however, my mom invited a big group of my friends from Stuyvesant over the house. I hadn't spoken or seen the majority of them since that day in the park after my biopsy, but my best friend Durwin whom I had known since we were about two, pretty much kept everyone filled in. There was a dozen or so that came to see me that day. Despite feeling like farewell, it was good to see them. We hung out, ate food and talked about miscellaneous things. We never talked about my being sick however. My friends knew I was and could tell I didn't feel well, but they appeared to be on eggshells and were afraid of saying the wrong thing. Even though our conversations reminded me of all the everyday goofiness I was missing, in the end, we basically did what teenagers do and it was great to feel like one again. While we were all in the living room, Durwin talked to my mom privately in the kitchen.

Mrs. Alotta, Danny's pretty sick huh?

He is Durwin, he has cancer.

But I don't understand how?

I don't either.

Truly I don't.

Is he...

Is he dying?

With that my mom and Durwin who she considered her second son began crying. They hugged one another and took a minute to regain their composure. At some point he rejoined the group. I remember saying goodbye to everyone when they left. I could see it in their eyes they didn't know if we'd ever have a day like this again. Truth was, neither did I. When Durwin and I gave each other a pound (slang for a hand shake) time seemed to pause. This was my partner in crime. We had grown up on the same block, in third floor apartments of adjacent buildings. When we'd want to play, half the time we'd scream at the other from the window as opposed to bothering wasting time picking up the phone. When that didn't work we'd often throw a rubber ball at one another's window from the street to get the others attention. Together we played little league, hockey, tennis, basketball, you name it. When we got in trouble it was usually together. One day I came home from nursery school with an envelope attached to a string that hung around my neck. Inside was a note from my teacher to my mom that explained Durwin had asked me for the enclosed $5 to be his best friend. Who knew it would be the best money I never spent.

Joy Juice

Alas, a few days after everyone had come to see me it was time. After all the tests, biopsy and of course the sperm bank that day had finally arrived. The posturing was over. It was a Tuesday morning in the beginning of December. A day that started like any other. I got up, had a good breakfast and got ready for my day. Believing if you look good you feel good, I put on some fresh duds. If nothing else, I would beat this thing with style. When it was time to go I grabbed my headphones and we were on our way. "Time for my Joy Juice!" I exclaimed.

Creating a nick name for chemotherapy was merely my way of making light of the situation. I do not know where the name came from as it simply seemed instinctive. Certainly there had been a lead up to this day but this was the true defining moment. Officially, it was Day 1. Whatever was going to happen, we were going to make this an experience to remember. Little did I know, at that moment I wouldn't need much assistance in doing so as my Joy Juice had an incredible personality that brought with it plenty of flare for the dramatic. We were off...

Overall, the ride to Dr. Brower's office was quiet. When we arrived at his office we greeted Laura and then I visited Nancy down the hall to have some blood drawn. Once this was completed it was game time. I walked back towards reception to say hello to my folks one last time before going into my room. We exchanged hugs and I was off.

Once in my room I went through my pre-chemo ritual of changing into my robe and weighing myself. Weight was a key concern as we were told that I could lose anywhere between 20 and 30 pounds. At nearly six feet tall and a slim 140 pounds, losing that much weight could prove disastrous. As I sat on the examination table taking in my surroundings and pondering the moment, I heard a slight knock at the door. "Come in." Dr. Brower entered the room and said hello in his mild manner that comforted you. Hello. It's such a simple word, but everyone that has had the pleasure of being Dr. Brower's patient, knows exactly the reassurance those two syllables would bring when he entered your room.

We talked for a few moments and he explained everything that we were about to do. We were a two man team and he was my captain with the knowledge of every road and situation that could potentially arise. His poise was unmistakable. Once he charted my weight and we finished our review, we were ready. He asked me to lie down on the table. As I began to recline I told him it was time for my Joy Juice.

Huh? He curiously replied.

Yup, it's time for my Joy Juice.

That's the nickname I've given chemo.

With a sense of approval, he shook his head and smiled.

We're going to give 'em our best, Danny.

I know Dr. Brower.

With that, Dr. Brower walked over to the other side of the room where there were two small refrigerators. The same kind college students have in their dorm room. My initial thought? Snacks! If it wasn't for the hazardous material stickers on the fridge, that might have been an appropriate theory. Wait a minute. What kind of nonsense was Dr. Brower about to give me? He removed a few clear pouches of fluid. One however, left an immediate impression as it was red in color. I guess this was the syrup and I was about to serve as the sundae. Each pouch was labeled ALOTTA. Alotta what? Alotta everything! That's my name, don't wear it out! As you can imagine, as a child I had heard just about every play on my last name possible. "Alotta everything" was the response I came up with one day that seemed to quiet all attempts at having a go.

Dr. Brower laid out each pouch of fluid in a line. Before doing anything he started an I.V. of saline solution with the purpose of coating my veins.

Ok, you're going to feel a slight pinch.

The I.V. was started. Despite not bothering me, I do have to watch intensely as a needle is inserted into my vein and if by chance I'm talking at that moment I always stop so I can focus. For all those who can't stand or despise them, Dr. Brower was a miracle worker. It was almost as if he slipped the needle into your pore and you never knew anything happened. As the saline continued to release a protective layer for my veins, Dr. Brower reached for the first vile of substance. It was the red syrup I had spotted moments earlier. Even though a great number of cancer patients receive their chemotherapy through a catheter, we opted to use my natural veins for two reasons. First and foremost, with a catheter comes the risk of infection as it's literally like having an open portal for infection to walk through. The second rationale was I had huge veins that you could drive a bus through. As long as my veins were functional it was preferred to use them.

Ok Danny, here we go.

The time had officially arrived. Despite all the tests and biopsy I was about to cross the threshold and officially become a cancer patient. I put on my head phones and pressed play. At that moment Dr. Brower injected my first round of Joy Juice into the tube that was carrying the saline solution and we were on our way. Apparently, if he were to inject it directly into my blood stream it could burn through me like acid. I actually thought this was an exaggeration, but down the road I would find out soon enough this was true.

Regarding those small refrigerators, chemotherapy is kept cold or at least mine was. Once it was injected, I could feel it travel the course of my body one vein at a time. It's kind of like a centralized brain freeze that travels up your arm into your core and back out again until it's finally warmed up by the blood inside you. It's quite surreal actually. Once the first vile was complete it was followed by three more that were equally cold. Already numb to the effect, they passed through without much notice. My first round of Joy Juice was actually quite uneventful. I had heard all these stories about how vicious an opponent it could be. Really? I wasn't impressed. Twenty minutes later Dr. Brower returned to the room and we were finished.

Ok Danny, we're done.

That's it?

Piece of cake!

Yes, you did great.

I rid myself of that awful robe and exchanged it for my fresh gear. Once I got myself together I rejoined my folks. When I got to the reception area, Dr. Brower was already there talking to them.

Hello.

How'd it go?

It was nothing!

Dr. Brower said I did great.

No sweat!

My folks and I said goodbye to Dr. Brower and headed home. I had a distinguished swagger in my step. It bordered on arrogance, but truthfully it was more confidence than anything. I felt like I had just taken everything my new foe had to offer yet I remained unscathed. I could do this. I had to do this. Better yet, I now knew what my new adversary had to offer and I was void of any concern. I was invincible, remember? If chemo hadn't gotten the memo, it surely had better ask somebody.

I sat in the back seat of the car on the way home. I was resting and at ease. There was a calm in the air, a sense of appreciation and accomplishment. Ahhh… As we drew closer to home something started changing inside me. It was unlike anything I had ever felt or known and I immediately knew that all those words of bravado back at the doctor's office were premature. I had always been taught by my folks to remain humble and never be conceited. Why had I acted so back at Dr. Brower's office? I had absolutely shown my ass and spoken too soon. Those last few moments of our ride were filled with regret for my earlier actions and I kept to myself. My opponent had surely pulled the infamous rope a dope and I was absolutely about to be served up for the dope.

When we arrived at our building my mom and I exited the car and took the elevator to the third floor. A certain mistake! We lived in a prewar building with possibly the slowest elevator in existence and I didn't have any time to waste. As the elevator crept to its destination my insides began to boil. Doing my best to conceal how I was feeling from my mom I tried to place my mind elsewhere as if that could stymie the inevitable. It was futile. Just as my mom opened the elevator door we had lift off.

That distinguished swagger I exhibited a short time ago quickly evaporated and that great breakfast I had that morning was no longer so great. I proceeded to make a colorful mess everywhere; in the elevator, hallway…uh it was nasty! With me trailing close behind, my mom rushed to open our apartment door as I spewed my "thoughts" throughout the hallway. I've always felt so bad about that day and the mess I made as my mom had to retrace our steps and clean it up. Sorry Ma!

The Tidy Bowl Man

As she opened the apartment door I immediately ran for the bathroom where I would have my first encounter with what would become my new best friend; The Tidy Bowl Man. Without exaggeration, I would spend the next six plus hours confessing my inner thoughts to my new comrade. My Joy Juice was anything but joyful. Where had this come from? Was I being taught a lesson for being so brash earlier?

If that was the case, I was sorry.

I take it back.

REALLY, I take it back!

Just stop.

Please stop!

I've learned my lesson.

I swear!

I promise!

What do you want me to say?

Just call off your dogs.
Please!

I heard a knock at the bathroom door. Equal part mom equal part protector my mom stood on the other side of the portal offering to help in any way she could.

Do you want me to hold your keppy? Keppy is the Yiddish word for head by the way.

No.

Do you want me to stay with you?

NO.

Is there anything I can do for you?

NOOOO!!!

In between each question and my outburst of NO was a chorus of unmistakable pain. She was being the great mom she is and I know she truly wanted to be in the bathroom with me that day but at that moment, this was my fight. My pleading to the Tidy Bowl Man and my Joy Juice continued to go unanswered. There was no amount of praying that could stop the onslaught. With each plea, chemo's wrath intensified. I knew cancer was dangerous and packed deadly potential but at that moment I wasn't sure which was worse. Cancer or chemo? The entire time I had been sick with my "flu," I hadn't felt like this. Never! Sure I had a high fever and was void of any energy but at that moment all of that felt like a walk in the park in comparison. What was this? This…. This was some bullshit! What sick demented individual created such a concoction? To add injury to insult, I was sure they either had gotten paid or were surely getting paid handsomely for their efforts. Are you kidding me? What kind of gig was that? Imagine the want ad for that position.

"Have an affinity for making people sicker than they've ever been? If you answered yes to this question then we have the perfect job for you." I wanted to take them and all their smiling sales reps and strap them down to make them feel what I was feeling. Wouldn't that be justice? Couldn't you imagine it? I know they were trying to help me, but at that moment it seemed like a reasonable request to literally give them a taste of their own medicine.

How's that commission feeling now eh?
Smile now dammit. Smile!!!

There would be no such retribution. This wasn't a lost episode of the long defunct series "The Equalizer." It was indeed prime time and I was the main attraction but instead my only audience, were my new best friends the Tidy Bowl Man and my Joy Juice. Apparently my performance was stellar as both continuously demanded more. Where was The Sandman from "Showtime at the Apollo" to pull me out of the spotlight and put me out of my misery? There was no such luck. My two new friends were insatiable. Rabid creatures I tell you with a thirst for the worst. If I had to compare them to a creature in the animal kingdom my new friends would be Hyenas. Absolute savages! They disemboweled me while I was still alive. By the time they were finished I was like a carcass on the Serengeti. They left me passed out on the floor in the bathroom cuddling up to my new porcelain teddy bear aka the toilet bowl. I had nothing left.

This routine would repeat itself every time I began a round of chemotherapy or cycle if you will. As time progressed my need to spend time with the Tidy Bowl Man heightened. His friendship was addicting.

Instead of longing for my friend solely when I'd return from the doctor, I began paying him frequent visits hours before leaving the house to receive my Joy Juice. As if my body knew what awaited, it began rejecting the mere thought of a new cycle. The deeper I traveled into my treatment the sooner my internal tantrums started occurring. Innocently they began with me merely getting nauseous prior to leaving the house for my treatment. Gradually the nausea was replaced with my paying homage to The Tidy Bowl Man practically as soon as I'd wake up the morning of a new cycle. The mere thought of what was in store the next day would make me anxious the night before. As if spending all day clinging onto the rim of a toilet bowl wasn't enough, these sessions with my new friend became the topic of my dreams. Sometimes they resulted in a restless night's sleep accompanied by tossing and turning making me nauseous as if I had motion sickness. There was no escape.

Oppressing the persistence of my new friend was impossible. He demanded to know all my inner thoughts and he would not be refused. The Tidy Bowl Man even had an equally relentless accomplice that came in the form of a small igloo cooler which I would have to carry with me in the car as we drove to and from the doctor. My confessions were accompanied by the sounds of an unmistakable orchestra. This was an ensemble of a different sort. Strangely I had gotten accustomed to the necessity of being confined to the bathroom but the car was an anomaly. While in the bathroom, it was you and your foe locked in battle mano a mano. I could deal with that. There was a strange tranquility in the knowing of your opponent and the arena in which the two of you would duel. In the car it felt like all fairness was out the window. The seatbelt would choke me as I'd lunge forward into that bucket. Without it, the violence of the moment would throw me into the seat or dashboard depending on where I was sitting. It was the worst. At home, at least the toilet held me up but in the car I had to maintain enough strength to clutch the bucket and balance myself simultaneously. It was debilitating and sapped every ounce of energy I possessed.

There I'd sit in the car next to one of my parents unable to control myself. From day one I had actually grown to appreciate the solace of being in the bathroom alone. In the car, not only did my poor folks have to listen to that non-stop ruckus, I know they could feel it. The car would shake violently with each thrust forward and then there were the sounds and naturally the smell. I reviled chemo for forcing this performance in front of them. It was disgusting and I was embarrassed. I know it was their pleasure to be by my side and truth be told each churn of my insides probably caused them more pain than it did me.

Stripped of all restraint, I wasn't even able to hold back once I got to Dr. Brower's office. I now required a bucket next to me while visiting Nancy as she drew my blood and as I lie in the examination room when Dr. Brower would administer my chemotherapy. He would be on one side of me injecting my meds while I'd be rolling to the other side spewing my thoughts. It wasn't pretty. Dehydration was a constant concern while undergoing chemotherapy and the more my two new friends demanded of me the worse it got. Dr. Brower had previously detailed some of the side effects but until I experienced them for myself no explanation could do them justice.

Once I was home I would literally sleep in the bathroom next to my new friend. The cold tile floor actually provided a certain level of comfort that enabled me to curl up and find solace as if I were in bed. When I would awake intermittently I'd proceed to hold on for dear life as if I were on the craziest loop du loop rollercoaster in existence. I would share my inner most thoughts with my new friend. Even when there was nothing left to discuss my Joy Juice forced the issue and demanded more. JJ was never satisfied and these were not "Good Times." How had I gotten here? Was this really to be my social life for the foreseeable future? I've always wondered what my mom did all day while I was in the bathroom. What if she had to go? I would be in there forever and we only had one bathroom back then. Did she hold it in? Visit a neighbor? Pee in a cup? I honestly don't know. Eventually the Tidy Bowl Man would get tired of what I had to say and I'd retreat to my bedroom where I would knock out from exhaustion.

With entirely no recollection of how I got there, I awoke in my bed at some point during the night. Groggy at first, it took a few minutes to clear the cobwebs and realize where I was. When I did, I heard the faint sound of TV off in the distance and light peeked around the corner from the hallway by way of the living room. I gathered myself and made my defiant return to the crime scene of earlier that day. I splashed cold water on my face. Having to pee, typically I was unable to stand as my legs were too weak and shaking. When I first started chemo this occurrence became commonplace but a few short weeks into my treatment it was different. At times I would attempt to get out of bed only to lie back down as I didn't possess the energy to stand. There was fatigue and then there was the fatigue brought on by chemo. Once I was successful in making it to the bathroom, I'd sit down and lean against the wall as if I would be unable to perform the task at hand without the additional support. Even when the job was complete I'd stay there for a few extra minutes in an attempt to gather myself and the strength required to pick me off of my perch. With one deep breath I planted my feet and made my way to the living room where my parents were watching television.

They had undoubtedly heard me in the bathroom yet they greeted me with a sense of surprise as if they hadn't seen me in ages. Following my first treatment I guess in some respect that was true. Yes I had taken a nap before and joined them while they watched TV but never after a round of chemotherapy. This was unchartered waters for them as well. My mom was the first to address me.

How are you feeling sweetheart?

I've always joked with my mom that sometimes she asks obvious questions. Despite the fact that I unquestionably looked like I felt neither my mom nor dad expected my response.

I'm hungry!

WHAT???

They were shocked. However, both of them started laughing instantly. *Leave it to you to wake up hungry after the day you had,* replied my mom.

It was great to share a laugh after such a rugged day. Nevertheless, despite my Joy Juice inspired all day confession, on that day and following chemotherapy injection days, crazy enough I would always be hungry upon waking up. When I did finally emerge from my bedroom, each time my folks would greet me with my traditional post Joy Juice meal. Sliced turkey breast and fake mashed potatoes with a touch of black pepper. I'll never forget that meal. It was so bland but it was all I could tolerate and after my marathon version of charades with the Tidy Bowl Man, I absolutely needed the nourishment. Completely exhausted, it seemed to take the same amount of energy to eat each slice of turkey as it took to crack open a lobster. One sluggish forkful and bite at a time I typically managed to eat barely a third to half of my plate.

On a different note, Dr. Brower had told me that being in such good physical condition was paramount to my being able to handle what was about to come my way. Therefore, as soon as I had eaten my fill and regained some strength I was determined to kick this thing in the derriere. I changed into shorts and a T-shirt and went into my parent's bedroom where we had some weights and exercise equipment. It was time to get in a post JJ workout. As I did bicep curls I continuously hyped myself up.

Okay chemo, is that all you got?

C'mon, show me something.

Don't you know who I am?

You can't beat me!

Clearly my distinguished swagger from earlier in the afternoon had returned and brought its friend modesty along for the ride. But you have to give me a pass. Remember, I was seventeen and invincible. In addition, having an athletic background supplied me with this hatred of defeat. Chemotherapy had unmistakably won the rounds earlier in the day but I was determined to rule the night. After forty five minutes of weights and calisthenics I was back to my normal self. Following a much needed shower I rejoined my folks and soon after fell asleep in what you now know has always been my favorite place, the couch.

As usual I absolutely had no clue as to how I got there but the next morning I awoke in my bedroom. After my morning routine I made my way to the kitchen where my mom greeted me with her overwhelming morning cheer. Quite possibly similar to mothers across the globe, she had the tendency to ask one too many questions prior to truly being one hundred percent awake but I supposed that's what moms are for. I might have been slightly groggy and still in my pajamas, but that had not affected my appetite. Hungry, I fixed myself an English muffin with butter and a slice of American cheese. Yes I had had chemotherapy the day before but on this morning, everything surely seemed to be getting back to normal. Not so fast!

My Pills

Partially through breakfast my mom informed me that it was time to start taking my onslaught of pills. In addition to receiving injections twice a month, I had to take approximately thirty pills daily. Shortly after

I would take my morning pills, Professor Stoddard would arrive and he stayed as long as my energy allowed. We were scheduled for school five days a week but there was at least one day a week where I wouldn't be capable of sitting up. Then there were the days despite being within two feet of each other where I would fall asleep as he spoke.

As for those lovely pills of mine, I don't know about you or anyone else for that matter, but I have never been an enthusiast of taking them. In elementary school I remember using M&M's when it was time to first learn how to swallow a pill. I didn't admire taking pills then and being required to take so many on a daily basis was anything but exciting. Having been informed that it would be best to take the pills with milk in order to coat my stomach my mom did the honors and poured me a glass as she knew I would never initiate the process.

Here you go sweetheart.

Sweetheart was her word. Since you're unfamiliar with my mom, she's quite possibly the nicest person you would ever want to meet. However, when she wanted or needed you to do something that niceness would absolutely drive me and my sister up the wall. She would put extra sugar on top when she needed you to do something. More often than not, she would add "At your leisure" to a request. Yeah sure, that meant she actually wanted that particular something done on the spot. Not that she truly wanted me to take the plethora of pills that she had just laid out in front of me, but she needed me to and she knew if she didn't actually watch me do so there was a possibility that I wouldn't. Truthfully, she was my biggest cheerleader offering words of encouragement.

I know it's a lot but you can do it.

That theory worked just fine until it was time to take Prednisone, which is actually a steroid that works in reverse. Instead of increasing and building muscle it unfortunately would break mine down. Was this a cruel joke? Have I mentioned I was nearly six feet tall and only 140 pounds? Now someone had come up with the bright idea of giving me a pill that would strip me of the little bit of muscle I had? Great!

Come on sweetheart, you can do it.

I know, I know.

The least they could have done was give me a steroid that builds muscle.
Instead I get the one that's going to make me look like shit.
Daniel Philip Alotta!

Daniel Philip Alotta. There it was. When my mom uttered your full government name you knew she had passed a certain point of tolerance. She was doing her best to work with me but she needed me to comply and take my medicine.

Okay, Okay.
Here goes nothing.

I reached for my glass of milk, picked up the first Prednisone, tossed one in my mouth and took a sip. Instantly I began coughing and choking. I nearly threw up at the table. I quickly rushed to the sink and spit everything out. I began rinsing my mouth out with water. My mom practically rocketed out of her chair.

What's wrong? What's wrong?
That might be the most disgusting thing ever.

There was absolutely no way I would be able to take several of these a day. I was beside myself. On only day 2 it appeared I was already facing an impasse. When I finally regained my composure, I returned to the table. There I sat staring at this pill that not only was essentially going to destroy my body but had the capacity to make me throw up as well. There was no way this was going to work. I could deal with the others, but this one just didn't sit well with me or my stomach for that matter. My mom could sense under the current circumstances there was absolutely no chance I planned to take the remaining Prednisone in front of me. In addition to having such an adverse effect on my body, taking it with milk was quite possibly one of the most repulsive things I had ever tasted. It literally disintegrated instantly upon placing a tablet in your mouth. Whoever had created a pill so appalling that it nearly made me throw up in my glass of milk clearly had a distorted sense of humor. Had they been picked on as a child? Did they have a disdain for society and this was their peculiar way of getting back at people? Whatever happened to a gel cap to make it easier to tolerate?

Despite the fact that everyone and all the instructions that came with the medication said to take it with milk, it was evident none of them had a clue what they were talking about. Had they ever taken the pill themselves? Absolutely not! If they had, they certainly would not have recommended milk as the preferred beverage to take it with. Clearly if I was going to keep my sanity and my breakfast I had to find another way. I poured some orange juice and tried again but it was equally disgusting. What was I going to do? For some reason I decided to try it again with orange juice except this time I took a sip of juice before I took the pill, then practically threw that nasty little thing into the juice that lay in the back of my throat and swallowed as fast as I could. It wasn't great but it was manageable and that was all I could ask for.

Although I know this seems like a small detail, having just spent nearly the entire previous day churning my guts out, the last thing I desired was a repeat occurrence because of a measly pill. Being able to conquer the task at hand that morning was a huge moral victory that would resonate every time I took Prednisone. All this talk of success was great but it quickly vanquished after I read the list of potential side effects that Prednisone brought with it. Was this a joke? I absolutely couldn't believe they were actually giving me this drug.

Prednisone Side Effects:

- *Difficulty controlling emotion / depression / mental confusion / nervousness*
- *Difficulty maintaining train of thought*
- *Immunosuppression / Infections*
- *Weight gain / bloating*
- *Severe joint pain*
- *Skin rash / acne*

What? Were they serious? This was just a handful of the side effects. All I knew was it had better do its task at hand otherwise I was without a doubt going to wind up way more screwed up than I was sick.

Chemo

Chemo. There are unmistakable signs of undergoing chemo and being a cancer patient. To the naked eye, a bystander merely sees the remnants of what was once a vibrant being. A deathly façade accompanied by a loss of hair are actually signs of being gradually consumed by chemo from within. As a young athlete who believed if I prepared for a specific challenge I could conquer any hurdle, there was no amount of practice that could make perfect here. Chemo has a singular purpose and that is to kill. Good or bad, its job is to destroy everything in its path and make no mistake it is extremely talented.

I continuously joked that I had no social life while undergoing chemo but in fact chemo was my life and my parents for that matter. Worse than any possessive significant other, Chemo was an unappeasable attention whore. It demanded and sapped all feasible energy from me and my parents. Exhausted might as well have been my middle name although I don't think Daniel Exhausted Alotta would have sounded as menacing when my mom riddled off my full name. It didn't matter where I was, sleep was on the menu. As a child I often fell asleep in my food. However, adding to the places where I found it acceptable to take a nap, it was commonplace to find me asleep on the commode during my journey. A typical sixty second trip to the bathroom easily turned into a thirty minute nap.

With words like exhaustion and debilitating describing what it was like to undergo chemo, anguish and torment would best describe what it was like for my folks to serve as front row spectators. Chemo might as well stand for slow death and watching me inch closer to that final destination was pure torture; a living hell. Each morning, my mom would come into my room to see how I was feeling and ask if I was hungry or needed anything. Once she had done so I would usually doze back off and she would get ready for the day's events. With chemo there was always an interesting itinerary. I would lay there in my bed floating in and out of consciousness. In the close distance, literally the room that bordered mine I would hear the shower running. Inside my mom stood seeking shelter and escape from her tormenter. Evidenced by the medley of sounds echoing from the tiled walls of the shower, such relief was unavailable. I could hear the water splashing off the walls of the shower as she pounded her fists against it demanding to know "Why?" Over and over again to no avail she pleaded for an answer.

Why?

WHY???

WHY???!!!

As if locked in competition I didn't know which was stronger, the flow of the water from the nozzle or her tears? Unquestionably the latter. Chemo might have eaten me from within but it undoubtedly did the same simultaneously to my folks. There is tremendous pain associated with chemo and cancer as a whole. The obvious involving the patient themselves usually serves as the main attraction. Conversely, it's the behind the scenes agony, the banging of fists in the shower, the beating into oblivion of a pillow in the bedroom, the wrecking of an office upon learning your child's fate that often go unseen and untold. Make no mistake these are without doubt the toughest moments of chemo. The orchestra that resonated from the bathroom each morning was proof that watching her child, her youngest, her baby was a deliberate agonizing pathway concocted by the most demented of villains. It's something no parent should have to endure.

Having been told prior to starting chemotherapy that I could lose anywhere between twenty and thirty pounds, my mom decided to take matters into her own hands immediately. Starting on the second evening and practically every subsequent evening during my treatment, my mom made me an ice cream shake. There was no way she was going to allow me to shrink down into the vicinity of 110 pounds. No way. As for me, I'm an ice cream fanatic so an ice cream shake every night was music to my ears.

The first week of chemotherapy was an interesting one. Within five days a few of the side effects of Prednisone began showing themselves.

For starters I gained five pounds in those first five days. You may be thinking to yourself "Wait a minute, this kid was eating an ice cream shake every night. Of course he gained weight." Although that was the case, let me provide you with a brief background into my metabolism. I was capable of eating anything and everything in sight without gaining an ounce. If my mom bought a dozen oranges, I ate them. Two boxes of strawberries...gone. Bag of chips...gone. My idea of a serving was the entire bag, box etc. Gaining weight for me was practically impossible.

To place some perspective on the situation, five pounds was more than I had gained between my junior and senior years of high school. Making matters worse, not only did I gain those five pounds in five days, but my entire midsection became distended. Instantly, I no longer had a flat defined stomach. Instead, if I cupped my hands I could now literally hold my belly in my palms. This may seem trivial, however, I can't stress deeply enough how witnessing my body change shape so rapidly truly messed with me. Everyone's self perception and confidence is extremely important and in less than a week I went from athletically defined, to no longer feeling comfortable in my own skin. Chemotherapy undoubtedly presented a tremendous chemical and physical challenge but at the moment it was evident that I had not considered the alternate battle occurring here and it was mental.

However, despite the physical and mental challenge accompanied by Prednisone, it's quite probable this same pill that I despised helped me stay alive. The taste may have been disgusting but our relationship was absolutely bitter/sweet as it made me gain as much weight in nine months as I had in the previous four years. That undeniably enabled me to maintain as much strength as possible during my journey. Had I lost 28 pounds as opposed to gaining them I would have weighed 112 as opposed to 168 pounds and that could have proved disastrous each time I got an infection when my white blood count (WBC) dropped to its lowest levels.

On a weekly if not daily basis it seemed another effect of my Joy Juice would show itself. Those initial five pounds increased gradually and so did my appetite. Truly it was astonishing. I was a ravenous beast. I ate a minimum of eight times every day. My desire for food was never-ending. Immediately upon waking up I would have my breakfast. Within two hours I would have a second breakfast. Two hours later it was time for lunch. By mid afternoon I was ready for another lunch. In between lunch and dinner it was snack time. Shortly after that it was dinner time. In between dinner and dessert there was some form of snack. Naturally, I couldn't wait for dessert as my ice cream shake became a highly anticipated tradition. Even during my sleep I wasn't safe as I started having the most vivid dreams about food imaginable. I recall waking up in the middle of the night craving poached eggs so, that I couldn't help but wake up and fix some toast and two poached eggs to satisfy my desire. I was an absolute junkie that fiend constantly for a fix.

I remember being at the table for Christmas dinner which in the Alotta house is a feast. As always, there was a multitude of courses but regardless of how many items were being served, everyone always saved room for the main event Spiedini. Why Spiedini? Although there is a Roman version made with cheese, the Sicilian version is made with your meat of choice and in our house that was London Broil. Sliced paper thin, each piece is dipped in olive oil and lightly covered with seasoned Italian bread crumbs. Then fresh tomato and sharp provolone are placed in the middle before it's rolled and placed on a skewer with a bay leaf on one side and a piece of Vidalia onion on the other. These steps are repeated until the skewer can handle no more. Then it's placed in the broiler until browned and crunchy on the outside yet tender on the inside. It is highly awaited by all those that attend Christmas dinner and everyone is clearly aware that it doesn't leave the house. That's right, they can take any and all the food home with them they would like but Spiedini is off limits! When I was around five or six, my mom's friend Susan found that out the hard way when I caught her trying to pack some to go. Shocked at the offense I was witnessing, I screamed. Maaaaaaa!!! Mom went on to explain to her that in fact she told me Spiedini was so precious that it didn't leave the house. Susan didn't leave empty handed but she exited without Spiedini. To this day that tradition still holds and guests are aware not to ask for it in their care package.

Okay, okay, I know I went off on a tangent but in my house Spiedini is a subject of extreme endearment and anticipation. Bringing it back to where I had started before I got carried away, there we were at Christmas dinner and everyone had had their first serving of Spiedini and now we were working on seconds. My appetite was voracious and when the serving dish came my way it looked like an appropriate portion to me and I placed the remainder on my plate. Appalled, my sister nearly launched out of her seat in objection. Sorry sis, I'll have to have you over for Spiedini dinner to make up for it. By the time I concluded chemotherapy, that initial five pounds ballooned to nearly thirty and at 168 pounds, I was a far cry from my starting weight of 140. Despite being overweight in my eyes and hating it, I recognized it was clearly better than the expected alternative of losing twenty eight pounds and resembling a concentration camp victim.

Gaining weight was the first of many physical side effects to reveal itself as a result of my new favorite medicine Prednisone. Without warning, I woke up with a pimple rash the likes of which I had never seen before or since. It started on the right side of my neck and extended all the way up towards my ear and the back of my neck as well. Eventually it spread itself to the left side of my neck and my shoulders and back as well. In the early stages of chemotherapy while my body was still capable of fighting infection the pimples would form white heads and being as anal as I am about pimples or anything else I felt didn't belong I would pop them instantly. As sick as it may sound, it actually provided a form of entertainment as you're well aware my social life was all but kaput. I know this sounds disgusting but ever since I was a young child it was safe to say that I could be described by my mom as a "picker." Now don't take that the way I think you might. What I'm saying is that if I didn't like something on my body and it could be picked off I usually did. On multiple occasions upon picking me up from nursery school or kindergarten my mom would spot specs of blood on the right collar of my shirt.

"Let me see your face!" she would exclaim. With her hand she'd turn my right cheek into her line of sight only to find that I had picked off the two moles on my cheek.

Daniel Philip Alotta!!! Uh oh, there goes my full government again. *You're going to give yourself skin cancer!*

Now I'm not sure if this is folk lore or simply a scare tactic parents use so that their kids don't do something as nasty as picking their moles off their face, but it never worked on me. Even to this day if I think a hair is out of place or I simply don't like something as minute as a pimple I usually get rid of it. My Prednisone induced pimple rash however, provided thousands of subjects at which to pick. As time progressed they became huge solid unpoppable masses. I remember asking my doctor why they had changed and it was then that I learned a pimple is actually a small infection or at least that's how he explained it. When your body is strong enough to fight it, it has a way of getting rid of it: alla the white head. Really? I couldn't help but think that was kind of gross. That meant I was walking around with a bunch of infections on my neck, shoulders and back. Yuck. As chemo took its toll, my body was no longer able to combat all the pimples that were sprouting. You might think that would have deterred me but alas despite the discomfort that came with it, as a picker at heart I found a way.

I recall getting out of the shower one morning and looking at myself and my rash in the mirror. There was one bump in particular that caught my eye. It was a solid impenetrable mass that lay in between my shoulder and the back of my neck. For some reason I decided that this offender was public enemy number one. I tried to squeeze it and the pain of doing so nearly dropped me to the floor. With my heart racing and my breathing sporadic and intense I took a time out to regroup. When I returned to the crime scene I gradually squeezed it from one side then the other. Over and over I repeated these steps as if I would be able to corner the offender and force it out. Then I managed to use two hands to evict the delinquent that had embedded itself in me. The pain was intense but I was determined and with nowhere to go but out, it happened.

WOW!!!

I nearly fell over! I could physically hear the skin crack open about a centimeter in diameter. When it did the thickest, nastiest clot of blood hit the mirror like a ball of wet cement. THUD!!! I nearly passed out. Maybe a slight exaggeration but my heart seemed to explode with it. It was beating a million times per minute. It was disgusting yet so cool. As soon as I regrouped and caught my breath the picker in me looked for another. Hey, try not to judge me as my social life had been limited to the doctor, the couch and the Tidy Bowl Man. You will be pleased to know that one "eviction" was enough as I truly couldn't endure that a second time. After cleaning out the wound and a wound it was, I joined my mom in the kitchen. Unable to stop the bleeding my T-shirt showed the evidence of my wrong doings. My mom was not too pleased.

Why are you bleeding?

What happened to your shoulder?

My explanation did anything but calm her.

Why would you do that to yourself?

You're going to give yourself scars.

As you may have guessed, it was only a matter of moments before she hit me with my full government…

Daniel Philip Alotta!

Yes ma?

Promise me you won't do that to yourself anymore.

Now in my house, a promise was as highly a valued commodity as a hug and even Spiedini and you absolutely didn't lie on a promise. I was caught in a conundrum. I couldn't lie to my mom but she was clearly beside herself over my picking episode. As politically correct as possible, I told her I would do my best not to do that anymore. Not bad eh? She always taught me that as long as I did my best that was all she could ask for. I don't know about you, but I thought that was fast thinking.

As week one progressed my distain for Prednisone grew. Despite knowing it was meant to help me, I resented that little pill and its group of friends. They seemed to be in endless supply. When it was time to return to the doctor for my second round of injections I was a bit weary but rest assured I was as humble as it got. My adversary had proven to be worthy and commanded the utmost respect. After my pre-chemo ritual of taking blood, Dr. Brower and I talked about the previous week before we got started.

Hi Danny, how are you feeling?

I'm fine thanks.

Last week sucked though.

I spent the whole day throwing up.

What in the world did they put in that stuff?

I'm sorry about that.

That's the Nitrogen Mustard.

The What?

The Nitrogen Mustard.

That day I learned from Dr. Brower that the M in MOPP stood for mustard. Mustard you say? Yes, mustard.

How in the world could mustard help defeat my cancer?

I liked mustard. How could it possibly make me so sick?

Well as I mentioned, this was no ordinary mustard. It was Nitrogen Mustard.

Nitrogen Mustard?

Yup, that's right.

The same Nitrogen Mustard that was used as chemical warfare dating back to World War I.

How had it found its way into my medical routine?

Apparently after World War I, doctors did a tremendous amount of laboratory testing with Nitrogen Mustard and found that it actuality helped with the treatment of lymphoid cancers, a category in which Hodgkin's Disease falls. There was one catch however. It was only safe to administer once every four weeks as it had the potential to cause leukemia if given more frequently.

Are you serious?

They were giving me something to cure one cancer that had the potential to cause another?

There we sat as I now learned a form of chemical warfare had been circulating in my body for the past week. I wasn't sure how I felt about that as it certainly seemed like a double edged sword to me but I trusted Dr. Brower. Either way, knowing why I was getting so violently sick was great and all, but it didn't make it or me any better. It didn't change or help the fact that I still spent the majority of my first day of each cycle hugging a toilet bowl. Nitrogen Mustard must be extremely efficient at its task because it is still used in treatment today. Once doc quelled my concerns we were ready to start round two. Right before we did he gave me quite possibly the best news I could have ever asked for.

Danny before we proceed I want you to know that the injections you're going to get today shouldn't make you sick.

Really???!!!

There's no mustard in this batch so you should be just fine in that category.

You'll be fatigued but there shouldn't be any vomiting.

You want to talk about elation. That news made me so happy that I almost couldn't wait to get started. I immediately assumed the position on the examination table and Dr. Brower once again walked over to the hazardous material refrigerators to retrieve a handful of liquid pouches. Similar to the week before, he started a saline drip in order to coat my veins. Once the saline was dripping for a few minutes we were ready. As I mentioned I had huge veins on my arms and the plan was to use the same vein from the previous week. As I would learn shortly, two rounds of injections was all the punishment each vein would be capable of handling.

Dr. Brower began injecting the chemo into the drip. This week I decided not to bring my headphones with me as despite going smoothly seven days earlier, the rest of the day surely didn't pan out the way I had anticipated. I figured I would try something different. Similarly my veins were interested in something different as well. The prior week it took a mere twenty minutes for my body to accept my Joy Juice. This time around it would take nearly forty five. Why the extra time? Dr. Brower explained that essentially chemotherapy was poison and not a natural substance for the body to admit. When your veins didn't appreciate something they would reveal that evidence by constricting and preventing the poison from flowing into the blood stream as a protective mechanism. Fortunately for me, I barely noticed as my uncanny knack of being able to sleep anywhere kicked into gear and I slept the time away.

When it was complete, Dr. Brower woke me up and removed the needle from my arm. We had accomplished our task. As I picked myself off the examination table there were no "That's it?" "Piece of cake" or "No sweat" comments as there were the week before. The bravado was gone and replacing it was intense fatigue. I was tired, truly tired. I got dressed and rejoined my folks who had been a bit concerned as to why things took so much longer this time around but Dr. Brower had already visited with them and soothed their apprehension. When I reemerged sans swagger it was evident to my folks that fatigue would be the feature presentation of the week.

Always cheerful and upbeat they greeted me energetically. When they asked how I was feeling they received my infamous one word answer.

Fine.

Much to my mom's chagrin, I was always good for one word answers. In fact at times they were the bane of her existence. After all, my older sister was as verbose as they came. She often drove teachers crazy with the number of questions she asked. When describing my aptitude for delivering one word responses my mom would always use the following example. She would explain that my sister and I could go on the same school trip and upon arriving home she would ask my sister how the trip was and she would all but write a thesis describing the day. Upon asking me how the same trip was she would get the following:

Fine.

It drove her absolutely insane and she would try her best to no avail to prod answers out of me. When I uttered my favorite word on that day, both my parents unquestionably knew there was no way I was fine. However, they had always taught me by example whether you win or lose you should do so with grace. It may not have been pretty but this was my attempt at doing just that. I barely remember the ride home that day as I only caught glimpses of it as my eyes intermittently peeked open. That afternoon and evening was much the same; a blur. Once I made my way through the haze and weariness of the day, my post Joy Juice meal awaited. Despite not laboring through an all day confession I was equally exhausted if not more than the week before.

The next morning I took my barrage of pills. We were in the second week of treatment and I was now confident in my routine. My mom had a chart to keep herself and all the pills organized. She was petrified that she would mistakenly give me the wrong medicine so she had each dose labeled in conjunction with the meal they were to accompany. By now I was accustomed to taking a sip of orange juice followed by the launching of Prednisone or any other pill into the juice that awaited. It's a habit that has remained with me to this day. The mere thought of taking pills with milk or water repulses me. It has to be juice and I have to take a sip first and then pop the pill. Any other order is too alien in nature.

There we were on day nine and it was becoming clear why we were only going to be capable of using each vein twice. We had started with the big vein in the middle of my right arm for the first two injections and on this day, when I looked down it was gone. Not literally, but it appeared to have imploded. What once seemed like a lifeline that protruded at least a centimeter was now flat and discolored. Instead of the green it once was it was now turning dark shades of brown. It was unlike anything I had ever seen. Usually enamored with such a spectacle this time around was quite the opposite. I actually loved my veins. I thought they were cool and marveled at how they would pop out when I exercised. I was a skinny kid and they served as proof that I could grow. Now one of my prized positions had vanished. Was I to be next?

That first vein would gradually turn from shades of dark brown towards closer to black in color. This progression would prove to be the fate for the remainder of my veins. Once a vein served as the main portal for chemo during a cycle it was finished. In the beginning each vein was capable of handling two weeks of injections.

As time progressed that decreased to one and at times none at all as I recall Dr. Brower inserting a needle one day to start a drip and I watched in amazement as my vein literally spit it out.

Not today! It proclaimed.

Even my veins had a threshold for pain and when they reached their limit of tolerance they too made a stand. Like Gandolf the Grey in "Lord of the Rings," they declared "You Shall Not Pass!" It was astonishing to watch actually. With each attempt, Dr. Brower would insert a butterfly needle into a vein and each time it appeared to ball up slightly as if serving notice that it was about to be evacuated. We even had to postpone my treatment by a few days on more than one occasion partially due to the lack of willingness on my veins behalf to accept their villainous tormentor.

One by one, each vein would implode, turn multiple shades of brown and then blacken. Not that I was prepared for these initial occurrences but I was totally ill-equipped by what followed. As if it weren't bad enough that my arms resembled the track marks of a heroin addict as opposed to that of an athletes, my veins hardened progressively over time preventing me from being able to straighten them without assistance. What was this and where had it come from? The culprit was Phlebitis and it was being served up courtesy of my new favorite acquaintance Nitrogen Mustard. Ah, Nitrogen Mustard (NM), there you are again. How many ways had you planned on enhancing my life? An answer it seemed only NM knew.

Getting back to Phlebitis, the hardening that I was experiencing in my veins was actually blood clotting associated with receiving NM. Without the use of saline prior to administering NM, it would literally burn through me like acid. Even with the use of saline, it would burn its way through each vein nevertheless. As each vein burned out and hardened I remember asking Dr. Brower why we just didn't use the veins in my legs as those were enormous. Apparently Phlebitis in the arms is considered Superficial Phlebitis which affects the veins on the surface. Administering chemo through the veins in my legs ran the risk of DVT (Deep Vein Thrombosis) which could result in the clots breaking away and traveling to my lungs which could cause death. WHAT??? How many additional conditions would we have to tolerate?

Sticking to the phlebitis at hand, it was making everyday life difficult. I placed warm compresses on both arms several times a day in what proved to be futile attempts to break up the clots. I walked around with what football announcers call alligator arms. This is when a receiver barely extends their arms when they attempt to catch a ball for fear of being hit by the opposing defender. I had no opposition preparing to put a lick on me yet my arms remained pined to my sides at nearly ninety degrees. This made maintaining a workout regimen practically impossible. I knew it was vital to maintain my strength but as I gradually deteriorated the only exercise I was capable of was walking from room to room and I wasn't capable of doing that particularly well over time either.

I recall playing basketball with some friends approximately mid way through my treatment. Upon grabbing a rebound a buddy happened to pull on my arm and I literally keeled over thinking they had torn my arm in half. This was Phlebitis at its finest. Each instance can vary but in my case it took years for the discoloration and hardening of my veins to dissipate. It was amazing actually. Almost instantly upon receiving an injection each vein would start deteriorating. One by one they shriveled up, blackened and hardened falling victim to chemo and its latest culprit. By the time we finished chemo, on the day of my very last injection, I only had one adequate vein remaining between both my arms. Despite being functional, it seemed keenly aware of what its brethren had endured and did its best to refuse the same.

With each attempt Dr. Brower made at inserting the needle, it shifted location in an effort to hide. Usually skillful at the process Dr. Brower appeared baffled. What usually took a matter of seconds, took him nearly ten full minutes. He kept prying and prodding hoping to secure entry into my vein. With each attempt it felt like he was trying to excavate it with that needle instead. Sweat began to pour from my brow and he repeatedly apologized as I began cringing from the pain. Again, again and again he kept trying. When he finally was successful, without a moment's hesitation my vein spit that needle out. Eventually he managed to do so again, and instantly taped down that needle a number of times in order to secure it in place. Despite being forced to accept this intruder my vein did everything it could to refuse its accomplice aka my Joy Juice. What originally started out as a twenty minute process months earlier would now take almost three hours. All my initial bravado from my first injection had long since faded, replaced by my "confessions" and passing out in the examination room from exhaustion.

Dr. Brower's office was small and there were only a couple of rooms, so the stubbornness of my veins would delay his entire day. Sometimes they would have to help me to another room in order to finish. I felt so bad that my parents would have to sit and wait so long. How much reading could they do? When I'd reemerge, I could barely walk. Despite having slept the entire time, all I wanted to do was get home and sleep some more. My veins had grown as tired and dilapidated as I was. Despite regaining their natural color for the most part, in most cases the destruction chemo rendered upon them was permanent as they've never grown back to their original stature. Although it varies from patient to patient, replacing them are a number of new smaller ones that seem to spiral in shape. Odd I know but it's true.

Currently, any time I have to give blood, finding a suitable vein on either arm remains a challenge. Like the heroin addict I once resembled, I have to tie a strap around my arm, pump my fist and tap my veins in order to make them surface sufficiently. One of my veins remains partially hardened to this day and if something or someone strikes the area, it shoots a pain that runs through me like nothing I know how to explain. The discomfort often prevents me from wearing a watch on that wrist. However, despite thinking about having it fixed I've never followed through on it because it serves as a sense of appreciation for life and my journey which I don't ever want to forget.

In addition to the burning and hardening of my veins I started noticing discolorations in my skin as well. When I asked Dr. Brower about them he explained that chemo had the same effect on my skin tissue. It was literally burning them from beneath the surface. On one instance while I was receiving my injection I lay in the room asleep as usual when Dr. Brower returned to check on me.

Hi Danny, how are you doing?

I'm fine.

Do you happen to feel any burning in your arm?

No.

Well I don't want to alarm you, but the needle has slipped out of your vein and into your skin.

Honestly I couldn't feel a thing. When I glanced over the side of the table at my right arm it had ballooned like Popeye's. Due to the red fluid flowing through my intravenous my entire forearm was lit up in the same fire red color. The skin that was being filled was clearly being seared at the same time. Somehow I managed to remain numb to the effect. Dr. Brower resituated the needle and my treatment continued. I closed my eyes again and that was that. That same spot on my forearm bares a discolored design to this day.

H & H.

H&H. No not the bagel company although that would have been splendid. Hemoglobin and Hematocrit. I had never heard these two words before and if by chance I had in passing, for sure I had no idea what they were or the information they could reveal. With every doctor visit I would have what's known as a CBC or Complete Blood Count. True to its name, it pretty much did what it sounds like. By taking blood and performing this test it provided a complete picture of what was going on inside me. Hgb and HCT as they were written on the test printout became true reflections of chemotherapy's wrath. They measured other issues but dehydration became one of our major concerns. Each element had an acceptable range of measurement and when their levels became elevated it was a clear sign of dehydration.

When you start chemotherapy you're instructed to drink a lot of water. Initially six or eight glasses sufficed. Gradually that amount doubled and it became commonplace for me to drink a gallon of water daily. Progressively a gallon became inadequate. The more my body thirsted for water the more dilapidated I became. It soon became necessity for me to drink two gallons of water a day. Doing so became an arduous task as it seemed as though I could never sit still. Which in reality was quite true as if I wasn't reminding myself to get up and grab a glass of water I could hear my mom's voice echo in the distance asking me if I needed a refill. Combine that with the fact that I now had to go to the bathroom constantly, it was a catch 22. If I didn't drink enough water I became more dehydrated and with that the more I fell apart. If I did my task, which I did, my bladder was constantly ready to burst. Instead of the dead to the world sleep I was accustomed to getting I now woke up a minimum of five times nightly to go to the bathroom. I was seventeen but I felt like I was 97 and ready for Depends. I could get up, go to the bathroom, return to my bed and within two minutes I had to go again. It was truly bananas.

For the sake of variety, I began mixing in some ice tea as water became mundane. If I went anywhere I did so with a cold thermos in tow. Eventually I kept a pitcher of fluid within reaching distance in my house as well. In addition to limiting the number of times I had to walk from my bedroom or living room to the kitchen, I also was now void of the energy to make those short trips. I drank so much my folks were concerned there could be a negative side effect for doing so. However, my Hgb and HCT levels continued to leave everyone dumbfounded.

My CBC reading when I was drinking a gallon daily showed both my Hs to be high. Despite doubling my liquid intake my levels worsened. How could this be possible? How much more could I drink? I guess I should have been thankful I wasn't asked to drink cranberry juice because as you know that would have been a major problem. Either way, I continued my two gallon a day regimen throughout the course of my treatment.

Dehydration didn't stop there however. Although in retrospect it makes complete sense, I had never thought about the correlation between dehydration and dry skin. The more dehydrated I got the dryer my skin became. There wasn't enough lotion in the pharmacy that could rectify how parched my skin gradually became. In between drinking my water I began applying lotion at least a dozen times a day. I've never witnessed anything like it before or since. I could literally squeeze lotion onto my body and without rubbing it in I would watch in amazement as my skin would devour it. Like pouring water on cement on a scorching day it vanished without a trace. Dr. Brower had clearly seen this before as he kept samples of lotion in his closet to give to his patients. He must have had an endless supply as each time I visited him he sent me home with several bottles.

In addition to my new friends Hgb and HCT we now had to pay keen attention to both my RBC and WBC standing for Red Blood Count and White Blood Count respectively. They have two distinct functionalities. Red blood cells essentially transport oxygen to your vital areas while your white blood cells are the primary defense for fighting infection. Similar to H&H, each one has an acceptable range of measurement. If elevated it usually means your body is producing a surplus in order to fight something that is wrong or abnormal within an individual which was the case when I had my first CBC prior to being diagnosed. If their levels are low it also means something is wrong but contrarily it reflects the bodies' incapacitation to fend for itself against infection. During the course of treatment all cancer patients are typically concerned with the latter. My case was no different.

Staying true to my earlier definition of Chemo (slow death), from month to month and cycle to cycle both my RBC and WBC declined gradually. Even though both measurements are important, as time progressed we became intensely focused on my WBC. In a healthy male, the appropriate range of white blood cells per cubic millimeter is between four and eleven thousand. Gradually my WBC would drop from double digits to seven then six then five and so on. As I mentioned it was acceptable to be in the single digits but once it started falling to three, two and then one it was serious cause for concern. Despite being extremely low when it hit one it was still relatively manageable. However, about two thirds of the way through my treatment I visibly looked like a hollowed out shell of my former self. Internally the picture was much the same as my WBC fell below one. At its worst it registered .001. To put that in perspective, let's remember that each whole number represented a thousand units. So a reading of seven actually meant 7,000 units. At .001, I only had one hundredth of a unit basically meaning the slightest infection had the potential to kill me as I was void of any internal defense. It was so dangerously low it caused us to postpone our injections on occasion for fear of irreparable damage. My off weeks to recuperate became increasingly vital to my survival.

It wasn't until we entered the fourth month of my treatment that we began to notice the most drastic changes in my body's defensive capabilities. It was at this point everything began to change from within me.

Bad Hair Day

We were nearly halfway through the gradual effects of chemo. With each day or week, some new ailment surfaced. I got all sorts of aches and discomfort that my wildest imagination couldn't have dreamt up. Although I didn't realize it at the time, in retrospect it's no wonder that all of these "things" began to occur in conjunction with the decline of my WBC. One morning however was more profound than the rest. Similar to every other day I woke up, went to the bathroom, brushed my teeth and headed to the kitchen. On the way, I passed by the mirror in the foyer and something caught my attention.

Damn, I look crazy!
Look at my hair.
What the hell was I doing in my sleep?

We gotta fix this.

Instantly I made an attempt to restyle the mess that lay atop of my head. And restyle I did as I wound up coming away with a huge clump of hair.

Oh shit!

Then another followed by another. I was barely touching my hair but with each movement hair was dislodging. I was freaking out. I looked at my shoulders and my shirt was covered with hair as well. I quickly retreated to my bedroom only to find that my pillow was also engulfed with hair. My world was spinning. It was three and a half months since I had started chemo and I figured if I hadn't lost my hair by then I was good. Yeah well, when it comes to chemo and your body there's no such thing.

I returned to the mirror in the foyer to re-inspect myself. If I simply ran my fingers through my hair it began raining down on the floor. I checked the little bit of mustache and beard that as a seventeen year old I regarded as a badge of honor and with a slight brush of my hand across my face the hairs began to fall. A quick check of my arms and legs revealed the same circumstance. I had never witnessed anything like it. If I did a jumping jack I would get showered with hair. It didn't matter what it was. Eyelashes, eyebrows, nothing was safe. Wait, not the uni-brow!!! That was my trademark. Not that I desire taking chemo again, but I sure could use a little help today combating the useless ear hairs that have begun to sprout.

From that day forward I would gradually transform from a kid with a thick head of curly hair to this wispy head of nothingness. So delicate, it was void of any style. It was just there. If the wind dare blow, my hair would resemble a wheat field that was caught at the mercy of Mother Nature's breath. I never went completely bald but I have to admit it was quite weird having straight hair. Admittingly losing your hair is easier for a man than it is for a woman but it was still an extremely awkward and defining moment. It marked a progressive downward trend in my overall ability to combat the side effects of my Joy Juice.

Even though when each moment presented itself, whether losing my hair, gaining weight or the addition of thousands of pimples, they appeared to be life altering in their own respect, in actuality they were the easy steps of the process. Carrying with them however, were distinct mental challenges that diminished my confidence with each new day. With the precision of a calculating captor, chemo methodically stripped away the layers of my self esteem one at a time.

Side Effects

First there was the weight and bloated-ness that in my opinion made me look sloppy and nothing like the athlete I had aspired to be. I know that gaining weight was better than the alternative and probably helped me keep my strength for a period of time but once it started piling on there was no stopping it. I felt like a foreigner within my own body. Each time I looked at myself in the mirror I didn't know who was starring back. Coming from a "hair" family, losing the majority of mine and having it go from thick and curly to flimsily thin and straight was quite the transformation. I stuck out like a sore thumb in my house. Hair in my family was a subject of pride and the envy of others and now I was without this jewel.

Throwing its hat into the ring of side effects were brittle bones. I found this out the hard way as I tried to keep athletically active as long as possible. One day while playing hockey I barely bumped shoulder to shoulder with another player. Paying it no mind as it was as basic a play as you could have in the sport I went about playing. The next morning when I woke up however, was anything but basic. I could barely lift my arm I had bumped the prior day. Off to Dr. Brower we went. An x-ray revealed that I had fractured it. Needless to say, that was the end of playing hockey. Chemo had managed to take away yet another thing.

Then there were the pimples, which to any pubescent teenager one pimple was enough to bring the earth to a halt. I had thousands, most of which were visible to the outside world. At seventeen, this wasn't a problem; it was catastrophic! I didn't want to be seen by myself let alone anyone else. They were so bad, that Dr. Brower sent me to a tanning salon to dry them out. However, this solution too was filled with potential danger as my skin could now burn in the shade let alone when exposed to direct sunlight or the equivalent. The poison rummaging through my veins was so toxic it could cause me to burn if I was next to a lamp for too long. Not that I made a habit of randomly standing next to light bulbs of course, but I've never forgotten when Dr. Brower warned me to be careful around them. That was definitely a new one on me.

I only used the tanning salon sparingly or when my rash was completely out of control. Consequently my complexion went from olive brown to Casper the ghost white. It was bizarre. Who was this visitor that now inhabited my body? Dr. Brower explained that chemotherapy was so strong that it had the capacity to physically change my genetic makeup. Curly hair; gone. Complexion; gone. Despite my hair regaining its texture, my skin tone has never recuperated. Post chemo when I have been exposed to a good deal of sun I have been burnt to a crisp a number of times which never happened before. Prior to chemo I used to walk around all year looking like I had a good tan. Now, not so much. In the summer, I used to feel like a sun god as my skin beautifully absorbed the rays without worry providing me with a complexion of envy. Although I have come to terms with these things as maturity has enabled me to realize the finality of the alternative, it took a period of time to mentally overcome them and their effects. During that time however, I had to figure out another way.

Void of the basic confidence that every teenager should possess I turned to fashion to make myself feel better. On one trip to Dr. Brower's I recall my folks saying why are you all dressed up? Where are you going? In general, I only had two places to go; Dr. Brower's or the couch. However, I told them "If I looked good, I felt good." They shook their heads and said "You're absolutely right." Whether it was sneakers, a shirt or merely a pair of socks, they did the trick.

Ironically, they didn't even have to be new. As long as they were fresh and looked good they put a smile on my face and gave me confidence. To this day one of my favorite things is a new or fresh pair of socks. There's just something about the comfort a plush pair of socks provides that puts me in a good mood. I guess it's no wonder two of my dresser drawers are completely dedicated to socks. I can't express the power and difference these basic items contributed to my daily struggle with chemo and cancer. It's a feeling I can't wait to share with other kids entrenched in their own battles with their own Joy Juice.

Although extremely important to me at the time, these hurdles at the end of the day were most importantly pain free. They didn't require any true physical effort to combat and in that way they were an extremely welcomed change in comparison to some of their brethren. During my journey, I developed gout so bad that even a pillow was too hard to sleep on. I used to ball up my comforter creating air pockets within and used that instead because it was the softest thing I could find. There would be times where it felt like a construction crew had been hired to sledgehammer all my joints and head simultaneously. I'd simply lay on my bed in shock wishing to fall asleep. It hurt to close my eyes yet the dehydration made me uber sensitive to light and forced me to do so. This susceptibility, brought with it migraines of unparalleled potency.

In an attempt to combat one malady I found myself aggravating another. There was no escape. The traditional raising of a window shade welcoming a new days rising sun was typically accompanied by pain and discomfort. I often lay in darkness praying to be sucked into an abyss. Was chemo turning me into a vampire? If so, where was my mystical strength? Little did I know there were super powers building inside me. They just hadn't fully revealed themselves yet but we'll touch on that later. I remember having to take this lozenge to combat gout that seemed like the size of a silver dollar. Probably an exaggeration but make no mistake, they were huge. As with any medication you were only permitted to take them so often but I wanted to take several in succession. In between doses I would consume prescription strength pain medicine for my migraines. For a kid that despised pills I sure was getting my fair share.

Generally, the superpowers I referred to earlier are not the unattainable sort we see in cinema. Instead, they are the ones that lie within that many of us don't tap until later in life. However, one in particular possessed similar capability to that of Wolverine from "XMEN." Okay, I know at this point you're probably saying "That's enough, he's gone too far" but it's true. As a result of chemotherapy, my sense of smell became absolutely insane. Upon arriving at Dr. Brower's on check up days I would often start getting nauseous because I could smell and taste the chemo that was being administered in the back. Incredibly the medicine had never broken the air. It was either inside its packaging or even crazier, inside another patient. The first time this happened I was sitting at Laura's desk talking to her before I went in to see Dr. Brower.

Danny are you alright?

I don't think so.

I think I'm going to be sick.

Hurry, take a candy.

Huh?

Trust me, take one.

Immediately I grabbed a candy out of the jar, unwrapped it and tossed it in my mouth. Almost instantly I started feeling better.

Laura, what just happened?

There's a patient getting their chemo in the back.

Yeah so?

Often, a cancer patient's sense of smell can get affected as a result of their treatment.

Sometimes you lose the sensation and things taste metallic.

In your case, you're experiencing the opposite.

Your sense of smell has been intensified.

Are you kidding?

Why else do you think I keep this big jar of candy at my desk?

I was stunned. There I sat in a chair at Laura's desk yet I could smell the poison passing through someone else's body. I wasn't sure how I felt about that. Kinda gross yet kinda cool at the same time. This newfound talent seemed to increase with time. Similar to Wolverine when he sensed a foe approaching my nose would often twitch in anticipation of an aroma. That was great if someone was cooking in my house but this capacity wasn't limited to good smells. My track teammate from college used to simultaneously marvel and get exasperated by this feat.

Hey Otis, something stinks.

Do you smell that?

No, I don't.

NO ONE smells it!

And no one is going to smell it for another five minutes.

I don't even understand what you're smelling right now.

We could be anywhere. Typically within a few minutes whatever it was would surface and he would catch a whiff. Good or bad it would usually unfold with me saying "I told you so" and him shaking his head in amazement. It was truly uncanny.

Now I don't know if there's any scientific fact or documentation showing the correlation between increased vision and hearing in relation to chemotherapy but I've always felt that both of these increased with my treatment as well. I remember taking my vision test for my driver's license and upon being asked to read the line I misinterpreted and thought I was asked to read the bottom line. When I did so the individual behind the counter was in shock.

What?

You can read that?

No way.

Read it backwards.

I obliged.

Are you serious?

Get outta here.

I had passed my test. Now this merely may have been a coincidence, but the same seemed to happen with my hearing. Years after I had finished my chemo I remember being in the hallway of a dorm as I prepared to enter my room. At that moment three people came up the stairs at the other end of the hallway (about 15 rooms away) and under their breath talked about my arrival.

I wonder if that's Lincoln's new roommate.

I yelled down the hall.

Yup, I am.

I'm Danny, nice to meet you.

The three of them stood there jaws dropped.

Holy shit!

You heard us?

I did, but I have really good hearing.

The three of them kept looking back and forth at each other. I waved at them and continued to enter my room.

Nice meeting you.

None of them knew what to say. Understandably, all of this could merely be coincidence as I always had good hearing and sight prior to chemo but they truly seemed to become enhanced courtesy of my new friend. If that was the case, I figured the least I could do was have a little fun with them. Unfortunately for my reflexes however, they didn't fare so well.

As each week of chemo progressed, Dr. Brower would take his triangular rubber hammer and test the reflexes on my knees and elbows. Despite holding on for quite some time, one day they just vanished. Upon taking the point of his hammer and striking the area of my knee and elbow that usually caused a reaction, on this day and all days moving forward during my treatment and for a while after, they were gone. He warned me to be careful around a stove as I could now burn myself and not realize. On the bright side he often joked it was a shame that I couldn't drink as he felt I could make extra money betting patrons in a bar that they couldn't find my reflexes. I never got to test his theory, as by the time I had another drink my reflexes had returned.

During my treatment, a couple of my friends, Walter who was from my actual high school and Chris who was a member of the rowing team I had been on visited me periodically. Walter and I had been on the tennis team together at Forest Hills and after practice on Wednesdays we'd always walk to the local bagel shop as they were half price. We loved those bagels and often devoured a couple of them as we walked towards the train station. Each time Walter visited he would bring me a half dozen everything bagels which we would tear up like old times. We would talk about practice, school and the happenings of some of my other friends.

As was the case with everyone on the rowing team, Chris was much older than me. At seventeen I was kind of everyone's kid brother on the team. We would go for walks every time he visited and at 6' 2", 225 pounds he would walk in front of me like a body guard making sure no one bumped into me. Most of our conversations revolved around music and sports. Talking with him enabled me to stay connected to a part of my life I missed dearly. Walter and Chris were good friends. Walter eventually would go off to college and Chris was training to make the national team. Combine that with me gradually not being well enough to accept visitors, the time we spent naturally drew to a close.

First Day of School

Due to my new friends Chemo and Cancer all life as I knew it came to a halt. I was no longer able to play sports, hang out with my friends or simply attend High School. I did my best to maintain as normal a life as possible but my sense of normal became altered. Despite having old routines replaced by new ones, I was able to graduate on time and attend my prom like everyone else albeit with doctor's permission. Both of these events are momentous occasions for a senior in high school. At the time, I was in the seventh month of my treatment which made it a little difficult to celebrate. On one hand I was thrilled to be with my friends. It was a victory of sorts as the majority of them hadn't seen me since I left school and it felt great.

As luck had it my prom fell on a recovery week. Despite being a shell of my former self, I boarded a bus with my classmates and girlfriend and headed to the Catskills as our prom was a weekend trip. It enabled me to temporarily taste what it was like to be a member of the senior class and afforded my girlfriend and me the chance to spend more than a few hours together which had become a rarity during my treatment. Instead of joining the rest of our class for daily activities, we spent the majority of the weekend in our room. Not that school let us have a room together but she roomed with my buddy's girlfriend and I roomed with him and then we all swapped. We shared a lot of laughter which had been missing from our every day. Like every other couple we got to put on our tux and gown and party like we didn't have a care in the world. The prom provided the opportunity to escape my reality and just be a teenager.

Graduation was slightly different. On one hand it was special to be able to walk and get my diploma with the rest of my class. Contrarily, as I spoke with friends they all talked about their future. Everyone's horizon included great summer plans followed by going to college in the fall. My invincibility or lack thereof, extended itself to the concept of time. When you're sick you no longer make plans two, three or five months down the road. It's not that you don't think that far, but getting through each day took about all the energy I had and the truth is I was just hoping to make it "down the road." I dreamt of a place where chemo, pills and all my new friends didn't exist. Going to my graduation was great but it reinforced that I was sick and incapable of doing the everyday things my friends took for granted, like partying the night of graduation and especially going away to school.

Instead, before I was well enough to go to Temple University, I enrolled in Queens College through the office of disabilities. They were incredible as they made sure I got my work, provided tutoring and informed my teachers of any difficulty that prevented me from attending. At the time I was barely strong enough to attend class but we quickly learned that if I failed to enroll in college, our insurance company had the right to drop my coverage. With that said off to school I went. Undoubtedly everyone's first day of college is a milestone. Something they typically remember. Mine was one I'll never forget. After all, I had recently reached two milestones having finished both chemo and my final CAT scan. Things were looking incredibly better. With each check up my progress had been phenomenal and I was continuously ahead of schedule. Collectively as a family, we may have been tired but we were elated that our nine month chemo marathon was complete. Strangely, when I arrived home early that afternoon from school, both my parents were sitting at the kitchen table.

Hello?

What are you guys doing here?

Talk about what?

Bad news for who?

Me?

At that moment, I already knew what that meant. I wasn't better. In fact it was just the opposite. But how could this be? I didn't understand. I had done everything doctors told me to do.

So what did they say?

A bone marrow transplant?

When?

Not until I wrote this had I thought about that day from my parent's perspective. After all, a child's first day of college is equally momentous for their parents. We had all gotten up that morning excited about our new horizon. However, at some point while I was at school and they were at work, one of my parents had to receive THAT phone call. But which one? Assuming it was mom I can't imagine how she took the news. Emotionally is a safe bet. Assuming? It had to have been my mom. Doctors always call the mom first.

Did she answer the phone at work when it rang? Despite expecting good news her heart would have dropped in anticipation. Upon finding out things were worse than ever, I think you would have to be in her shoes to understand. How was she able to gather the strength to call my dad and tell him? What was that like? How long was the conversation? Knowing my dad and the relationship we have, he was surely in a world of hurt when he got off the phone.

Were they both left to themselves in their own moment to find a way to cope? How did they do so? What motivation did they use to gather themselves and deliver the message to me? That's when it hit me. **ME.**

However, I learned that THAT call didn't come on my first day of school, it came late afternoon the day before. My mom was at work eagerly awaiting Dr. Brower's call. Despite being rummaged by chemo, I had responded incredibly over the course of my treatment and at each check point I was vastly ahead of schedule. When she picked up the phone and heard Dr. Brower's voice her heart began palpitating.

Hello?

Hi Mrs. Alotta, this is Dr. Brower.

Yes?

And?

Mrs. Alotta, I don't know how to tell you this.

My mom sank in her chair. Shaking, she began to cry.

Mrs. Alotta, Danny's CAT scan showed that his cancer cells are bigger than they were originally.

At this point she was distraught. The only thing keeping her intact was her quest for information and an explanation.

How is this possible?

He was doing so well.

I don't understand!

Mrs. Alotta, this is totally unexpected and I wish I had an explanation.

Void of the explanation she desperately sought, my mom's search for answers led her to the bathroom down the hall from her office where she began screaming and banging her fists on both the walls and sink. She was enraged. No matter how hard she beat the counter, her efforts were futile. She was so loud in fact her friends from work heard her down the hall and came running into the bathroom where they tried to hold her as they were afraid she was going to hurt herself. Even though the news she had just received was regarding my fate, she didn't know if *she* could survive. Her bathroom rampage didn't provide any solution either. At that moment even one of my one word answers would have done the trick. It wasn't to be. If she was going to find solace, it was in that all too familiar phone call she had no choice but to make.

Knowing everything had been going according to plan, my dad was upstate visiting the Schedivy's for a couple of days. Anticipating our results any day, once he heard my mom's voice he knew we had received anything but good news.

Phil.

What's wrong?

My mom started crying as soon as she heard his voice. Knowing the sound on the other end of the receiver wasn't tears of joy, my dad followed suit. At the patio table when the call came the entire Schedivy clan knew what his reaction meant.

Tell me what's wrong!

With every word his response intensified. Demanding answers, my mom was unable to supply them. All she had to offer was the fate which we now faced. In an attempt to soften the blow Ray put his arm around my dad. My dad was ready to drive home immediately but my folks decided based upon the time of day it would be best to do so the following morning as it was a long ride. When they hung up the phone my dad fell into Ray's arms.

Back home my mom now had to face me. My folks had decided they wanted to give me the news together. Often in amazement of my mom, the composure she displayed that evening leaves me awestruck. We had dinner and watched TV together yet she never let on that anything was out of the ordinary. Meryl Streep may have won the Oscar, but who was the "Iron Lady" now? No amount of coaching could have prepared her for her role that night. I can't imagine the thoughts that pierced through her as we sat next to one another on the couch. Only one word can summarize her poise. Strength!

My dad arrived home early the next morning. Unbeknownst to me when I left for school, my parents had an appointment with Dr. Brower to discuss our situation and what had gone wrong. Unable to provide an answer to the latter they covered every detail of our next steps with meticulous precision so they could relay them to me and answer any questions I might have. Despite all their preparedness, they seemed a bit uneasy when they asked me to join them.

So there the three of us sat at the kitchen table and my parents explained that I did need a bone marrow transplant but first I had to have another operation to dissect my cancer cells and find out... well...something. During the course of taking chemo each patient has to take periodic CAT scans. My latest scan had shown that instead of my cancer being gone it had grown worse than it had been originally. We talked things through and despite it being emotional I remember telling my mom and dad it was ok. I could be totally wrong, but I don't even think we ever turned the lights on in the kitchen that afternoon.

Despite a few prior steps, preparation for my transplant was to take place rather immediately. However, a bone marrow transplant is quite an intricate procedure. First thing they would have to find was a bone marrow donor. They preferred to use my own as typically an individual's body would accept what was naturally theirs. It would have to be harvested and "cleaned" prior to being able to put it back. If my own marrow didn't take they would try my sister's as siblings have a high likelihood of being a match. Potentially, my parents would have been next even though the probability of parents being a match, are much less. All the while I would remain in a bubble so that I wouldn't be susceptible to infections from the outside world. Sounds like "Bubble Boy" alla another episode from "Seinfeld" (okay okay so I'm a fan of the show). Oh yeah, did I mention at the time the transplant would cost between $250,000 and $500,000 dollars. WHAT???!!!

My Sister

We certainly didn't have that kind of money and bone marrow transplants were not considered normal procedures back then and therefore not covered by our insurance. What on earth were we going to do? Upon learning the news, my mom called my sister who had recently returned home from college, to let her know. As if the transplant wasn't daunting enough, the price tag presented an unattainable challenge; a conundrum indeed. My sister who was always reassuring told me that despite the struggle we had already endured and the bumps along the road that came with it, that was the first day she believed I was going to die. There it was, her little brother was on the way out. She lives in Brooklyn now and is the executive director of a nonprofit. When we were kids, we created a duet called "I'm a little Brownie Puppy." Alas it appeared our duet was poised to become a solo.

As a family, collectively we were in unchartered waters with me, but as an individual each step you took was new as well. Your parental support system got stripped from you overnight and I'm sorry for that. Undoubtedly if you had an issue or concern that under normal circumstances found the ear of mommy or daddy, were you left to figure things out on your own or with the comfort of friends as opposed to family? It was unintentional but how did this make you feel? They were in crisis and I got all their attention, did that translate to you as me getting all of their love as well? Did you feel alienated? You were their first and I was their baby. Did they love me more? No. They cherished us both but they were just trying to save one of their children and in the process might not have been able to tend to the needs of the other. Had you fallen ill, all these circumstances would have been reversed but it wasn't and my getting sick was unfair to you.

Somehow that flip of the coin was our destiny. Chemotherapy left its scars on all four of us. As a family we often express ourselves through food but we're all no strangers to the pen. I always appreciated the poem you wrote about our journey when I was sick.

Circumstantial Evidence

The cost of living in a city
like New York
in a country
like America
can vary from moment to moment.
Circumstance can dictate
the dollar value of a life.
In the case of a
seventeen year old
brownskinned boy
you need to figure in the cost
of a new pair of sneakers
every six months
an occasional movie
and enough lunch money to support
a soon to be six foot frame.
Let's say for the sake of argument
we give him an additional characteristic.
Behind his brown sugar eyes
past that mess above his lip
he refuses to shave
circulating somewhere
in a body that
stays out past 3am to be bad
suffers through math class
and has recently discovered love,
there is a small world of blood cells, platelets
and lymph nodes.
Do you know about lymph nodes?
Well, when something fucks them up
like pollution or nothing
they change,
and now that boy has more than he started with.
He has cancer.

If that boy is your brother
my baby brother
I need to figure in the cost of a lot more
than medicine
who's gonna pay for the Kleenex
for the phone calls
the long distance calls that haunt me
I let the machine get it
I can't bare another
let my machine get it
over and over again.

Twenty four hours ago
still a boy brother son
not patient.
Patience have patience
just sit tight you will get yours
one day.
word hard harder hardest
you can do anything if you set your mind to it
in time
wait
for biopsy results
hair to thin
mark each pound lost
as space between treatments
days become prayers answered

No one asked how I was doing
how is your mother
difficult for her
I cannot
ask for help
have a hard time
cannot fuck up now

I have fucked up
enough
who is going to clean up after this mess
the role of the good ambitious smart
too smart daughter
I come home on winter vacation
sometimes on Thanksgiving
until we stop pretending we could afford it
I was cleaning houses
for my professor
who teaches art and social change
fosters discussion of activism
amongst her colleagues and students
call her by her first name
still
she gives me a key to the back door
shows me where to scrub
and watches.

It is August
they use the last vein they were saving
for this moment
they pump the poison
that has burnt up all the other veins
now hardened
so it is difficult for him to bend his arm
he wears these badges
of his holocaust
feels the urge to vomit
but will not
because he wants to savor this moment
because he wants to be brave
because if this shit doesn't kill him
nothing will
because he doesn't want to upset his mother.

In the taxi on the way home
he can no longer fight back
nine months of chemical warfare
intended to exorcise him of
the whisper in his ear
that will not let him sleep
for fear he might lose control
at just the wrong moment
so
he wretches a perfect picture of
our reality all over the floor of the cab
but its okay
he's still brave

On that day when my sister received mommy's call telling her I needed a bone marrow transplant, she did the only thing she could think of. She placed a call to her best friend's mom who was in public health, who gave her information on potential financial assistance for my bone marrow transplant. She reassured my sister not to worry that she would help figure this all out. Knowing the possibility of help existed provided extreme comfort to my folks and helped ease some of their distress. My sister was still looking after my next step just the same as when we were little.

Dr. B's Office

The next day we were in Dr. Brower's office where he explained everything from the bone marrow transplant, to the operation I was about to have to the new type of chemo I would require. Despite understanding everything he said it was all a blur. Although he had just spent part of the previous afternoon with Dr. Brower, my dad continued to refuse the thought of our predicament.

Dr. Brower, what are the chances that Danny's CAT scan is wrong?

Less than 5%.

Even though this was the third day that my folks had been dealing with the news, having Dr. Brower state those odds seemed to deflate them further. It was almost as if they were reliving the day we met Dr. Brower and he levied our predicament for the first time. There was no escaping so we were just going to have to come together and fight again as we had before. When all conversations were finished, I asked my parents to let me talk with him in private. The contents of that conversation I've never told them until now.

I don't understand doc.

I did everything I was asked.

EVERYTHING!

What did I do wrong?

I'm tired Dr. Brower.

I'm really tired!

Danny, you didn't do anything wrong.

I wish I had a good explanation but I don't.

This is totally unexpected and I'm sorry.

I know you've heard this before but we have to act fast.

This is just crazy to me.

What if I said I don't want to do this anymore doc?

Where is all this coming from doc?

Please tell me, what did I do wrong?

Danny, this isn't your fault!

Don't think that for a minute.

But please listen to me.

I say this to you as if you were my son.

We can beat this! And we're going to do everything we can to do so.

I know doc, but I really am tired.

What…What if I just don't want to?

Danny, that's not option here.

If you don't do this, we won't be sitting here this time next year having a conversation.

Huh?

Danny, without this you'll have a year or less to live.

A year to live?

Oh…

Those words hit me hard. I paused for a minute as if to digest the clarity of what had just been said.

Since you put it that way, when do we get started?

It was possibly one of the briefest conversations Dr. Brower and I ever had but one I'll never forget. What else do you say to someone when they tell you, you could be gone in a year. It truly leaves an everlasting impression. I shook Dr. Brower's hand and left his office. When I rejoined my parents in the waiting area, I pretended I never heard those words. Seems like putting on a façade in the face of daunting news runs in the family.

Game Time

Prior to scheduling a bone marrow transplant, I had to have a laparotomy. Basically this is a fancy name for cutting open my midsection and taking samples from every organ from my pelvic area to my neck with the exception of my heart. The wound would take about 25 staples externally and countless dissolvable stitches internally. As you already know, athletics are my first true love but contrary to everything the discipline of sport had taught me, there was no amount of practice that could have prepared me for this day. This was my Super Bowl and it was anything but ordinary. Once I had my uniform consisting of that lovely green robe and footsies with the cool grips on the bottom I was left alone with my thoughts.

Hey God.

Guess this is it huh?

If it's all the same to you, I really don't want to die.

Not sure if you're listening, but we could really use a little help today.

At that moment there was a knock on the door, similar to the knock on a locker room door when they're ready for a team to enter the stadium. I closed my eyes and offered myself a few words of encouragement.

C'mon young fella.
You can do this!

I planted my feet, stood up and walked towards the door. My first few steps were a little wobbly. As I grabbed the handle on the door I stabled myself. On the other side awaited a nurse ready to take me to my destination. We seemed to move in slow motion down that cold dark corridor. Each step was slower than the next as if I was strategically plotting my escape. This time felt unlike my previous journey. It no longer seemed like part of a new adventure. Somehow that youthful ignorance I had started my journey with had evaporated and I was now fully aware of the gravity of the situation.

Gradually we inched towards that light peeking through the window of the door down the hall. The bright lights were present but where were the cheers? It might have reminded me of a sporting event, but there were no sponsors or fans for which to perform. It was merely me, the doctors, his team and my family in the waiting room. We pushed open the door to the operating room. It was just as cold as I had remembered, but this go around there would be no reference to George from "Seinfeld." It was all business. When I walked towards the operating table I spotted a familiar face.

Hey Dr. Clarke.
Hello Danny.
How are you doing today?
Fine thanks.
Good, we're going to figure this out.

Just as it had been previously, his response was good enough for me. Upon meeting him nearly a year before Dr. Clarke had passed my little test. On that day as I had done before, I trusted him to lead me once again down a path I had never been. He walked me over to the operating table and helped me get comfortable. With the addition of a blanket covering my feet and the rest of my lower half that cold room began to warm a bit. All of a sudden this began to become familiar. Similarly to my previous OR visit there were a bunch of people doing whatever it was they were doing and I once again assumed they were doing it well.

As I lay there taking in my surroundings, I noticed the tray to the right of the table. It contained several scalpels and pieces of medical instruments. They presented a clear image of why they had arrived at the "show" that day. They were there to do damage and get to the bottom of things. Just as my mind began to get the best of me, someone came over to start an IV and clean the area of "interest." Once that was done, Dr. Clarke rejoined me at the table for a little pre-operation schmoozing.

Everything okay?

Yeah sure, besides the fact that you're about to cut me open and give me 100 stitches, I'm feeling great!

You're going to do just fine.

In a calming manner, he reviewed exactly what we were about to do as he outlined the area with a marker. He did his best to put me at ease. In came the anesthesiologist who just as I had recalled talked to me for a few minutes to let me know what they were about to give me. It was as democratic as I had remembered. This time was going to be different however as I was going to have general anesthesia that would knock me out completely. Instead of 90 minutes, this time my operation was scheduled to take somewhere in the range of four hours.

Once all the semantics were out of the way I started my countdown from ten. My chemo inspired bloodhound senses kicked in as I could taste and smell whatever he was injecting in me. However, just as the taste began to disgust me I was out cold. I guess some things never change as I don't remember counting past eight. Hopefully, everyone had placed their bets in time. Contrarily, I did not talk Dr. Clarke's ears off nor did I begin to feel anything during the procedure this time around.

For me the next few hours flashed by in what seemed to be couple of minutes. One second I was asleep in the operating room, the next I was in recovery. For my parents on the other hand, each minute seemed to last an hour. When he wasn't pacing back and forth my dad was wearing a hole in the floor tapping his foot. He does that you see when he's anxious about something. On this day, his nerves reached a pinnacle. My mom on the other hand read voraciously to keep her mind occupied. However, every time a doctor walked into the waiting room their attention sped toward the entering figure at the doorway. Time and again the doctor was there to deliver news to someone else. If you know the confines of a waiting room, the quarters are quite close thus allowing everyone to hear the news being conveyed. More often than not, the news other families received was not good which heightened my parent's apprehension. They couldn't take it anymore. With each doctor's arrival the sorrow in the room became an emotional burden.

Then it was their turn. In walked Dr. Clarke. My mom grabbed my dad's hand. Their hearts began to pound. They stood immediately. As he walked towards them it was as if they could watch my life pass before them. My birth, childhood, the sandbox, running around the playground, little league, picking me up off the couch and putting me to bed. They couldn't help but wonder if we had staged our last act.

Hi Dr. Clarke.

Hello.

Would you like to take a seat?

Why was he asking them to sit? Was it that bad? The three of them turned their chairs to face one another. My dad couldn't take it anymore.

So?

This is just preliminary, but I just had my hands in each of your son's organs and I don't see any cancer.

WHAT???

Does that mean he's okay?

No.

It provides us with a ray of hope and it's obviously better than the alternative, but please understand without the pathology this doesn't mean anything.

So what now?

Now we wait and hope the pathology report shows the same.

I wish I could tell you more.

Other than that, Danny is doing fine and he's in recovery.

You can see him shortly.

Thank you.

With that they shook hands and Dr. Clarke exited as quickly as he had arrived.

Before I knew it, the recovery room spotlights were blinding me as I made my first attempt at opening my eyes. Combined with that infamous beep beep beep, I started becoming reacquainted with a familiar scene. Just as it had happened before, once I fully opened my eyes I was comforted by the fact that someone was there to greet me. How'd they do it? Where were they hiding the sensor that told them my eyelids were opening? Who cares? I didn't, and I have to suspect that everyone that has ever awoken in a recovery room feels the same. Keeping with tradition, before I knew it my mom and dad were there as well. As I had suspected last time around, it was a party but no one got my memo regarding the Carvel ice cream cake with the crunchies. Oh well.

At the point when my parents and nurse started asking questions I finally realized I had had surgery. Each time they spoke I tried to respond but the tube down my throat made it extremely difficult. When I would attempt to talk, you'd hear this intensely annoying suction sound followed by drool falling out the side of my mouth. As I took in my surroundings, I realized that I had tubes everywhere. My nose, mouth, arm. I even had tubes I didn't know about yet, but that's another story. It seemed like every time I took a breath, that crazy suction sound would ensue followed by this crazy looking brown stuff flowing through the tube that was in my nose. The fluid would flow into a container that had to be measured daily to make sure my body was getting rid of unwanted fluid in my lungs. I don't know about you, but to me that sounded nasty. Yuk!!!

Once it was confirmed that I was officially recuperating, it was off to my room. This is where I have to give a special thanks to my doctor's because it wasn't until a couple of years ago when I visited my mom in the hospital that I realized everyone doesn't get a private suite. Truly, my room was amazing. It had hand carved mahogany walls, eighteen foot ceilings, a view of the river, a huge private bathroom and enough room to sleep six. Without exaggeration it was bigger than some of my friend's apartments. It was great. Honestly, it never dawned on me even as I took walks in the hallway that this wasn't a normal room.

Spending time in the hospital is interesting. If you learn one thing, it's who really cares about you. I'll never forget when my cousins Joan, Marvin and their son Billy came to visit. Joan and Marvin arrived on one day and Billy came on another. It was great to see them despite not being able to communicate very well. My cousin Billy brought gifts: new sneakers. I can't tell you what this gesture meant to me at that time. You're laying there without a clue as to what the future holds and something as simple as a pair of sneakers changes all that. This is the core of what Joy Juice means.

Most importantly, was the support that cousins Joan and Marvin brought to my parents. During their visit, everyone remained strong in my presence. When it was time for my cousins to leave, my folks walked them out. Once everyone was outside the room, the strong facades fell and emotion poured. I was bed ridden, but the window on the door was my portal to the outside world. As the door closed behind them I stared intently through my window. No sooner than the door found its place against the frame, I remember watching my mom collapse in cousin Joan's arms as they said goodbye. I did everything I could to sooth her sorrow.

It's ok mommy!

I'm going to make it!

I promise!

Please don't worry!

I did my best to scream and tell them I would be ok but nothing came out. I was temporarily mute. Instead that damn tube caused me to choke on my own saliva. For days I struggled to talk so, that I had to write down all my conversations. Each attempt to talk would be accompanied by uncontrollable drool. My dad gave me his handkerchief to combat this new nemesis of mine. When you have tubes down your throat, you're not allowed to drink water as it will cause you to choke. Therefore, my folks and I would use a lollipop sponge to water my lips in order to prevent them from cracking. So there I was, drooling out of the side of my mouth as I wrote down all my conversations followed by a dapping of my lips with a lollipop sponge. It was not a pretty scene. I still have the majority of those items as they are testaments to how fortunate we are.

Tube Talk

Every battle has its defining moments. For this particular hospital stay it was the "Taking of the Tubes." On the first night of my stay, I lay asleep when a nurse entered the room. I was groggy and numb but sensed her approaching.

Hi Daniel, how are you?

Before I could respond she was reaching under my blanket for my "situation."

WOW!

What a hospital!

They really make sure you're taken care of here.

Wait a minute, I can't feel a thing!

What have they done?

What happened to my…

Next thing I knew I felt this strange pressure coming from my midsection and my Johnson. And believe me, it was not the most pleasant feeling you want to have coming from your Johnson.

What's happening?

Shit was really becoming extremely uncomfortable. Then before I knew it…POP! The nurse was holding this tube that as I remember it, was a couple feet long and the opening was at least as thick as my pinky.

Are you kidding me?

That came out of where?

How the hell did you get it in there?

I mean, when?

Whew, thank God I was asleep.

The experience was about all I could take at that moment because within a few seconds I was out cold. And this was only the first night.

Bright and early the very next morning, Dr. Brower was in my room shortly after five a.m. I always marveled at this because I knew he started seeing patients in his office around nine. His dedication was amazing to me as I surely wasn't his only patient but he was there every morning without fail. If there was a handbook on what a doctor should be Dr. Brower certainly wrote it. While in my room, he would review the notes on the clip board at the foot of my bed and we would talk briefly about how I was feeling. His compassion was incredible. Shortly after he arrived he left to visit other patients. Later that morning a different nurse came to see me.

Good morning Daniel.

It's time to get up and go for a walk.

Absolutely, let's do it.

Wait wait, you have to learn how to get out of bed.

I attempted to get out of bed but nothing happened. Only my arms and head moved slightly. I felt so silly. Getting out of bed as I had known it was futile. That moment was the first time I realized I had been cut open. It's quite humbling actually not being able to perform such a basic task. It was time to go to school. The nurse instructed me on proper technique of how to get out of bed and stand up.

First thing first was locating the remote control attached to my bed. When I first saw it, I had wondered what it was for. With a touch of a button it propped me up so that I didn't have to waste energy trying. This was brilliant. Despite not having to expand energy, as the bed moved forward, my abdomen made it clear it was not too happy. The next step in the process echoed this dismay as I had to use both hands to get each leg off the bed and onto the floor one at a time. WOW. It sure is ironic how we don't appreciate our basic functions until they are stripped away, although be it temporary in this case. Once I managed to get my feet on the floor it was time. With one hand on the rail of the bed to my left and the other on the rail to my right I attempted to lift myself off the bed and stand. Yeah right, not so fast. It took three times in all, so I guess three times really is a charm.

Standing was great as I hadn't done so in over a day but then I had to manage to walk. First was the right leg. I guess instinctively we always lead with our dominant side. However, it was anything but dominant. Quite pathetic actually. Firstly, I don't think I even picked my foot off the floor. If I was lucky, I slid it along a few inches. Small slide after small slide I was on my way. Next thing I knew I was walking. Well sort of or at least that's what I'd like to call it but it was definitely more like hobbling along. In tow was my IV and that damn thing seemed to go everywhere with me. Interestingly enough it was good that it did as similar to a crutch it stabilized me. Several times a day this would become my routine. Gradually, I became confident in my stride. Eventually I resented that damn IV pole as it slowed me down. While on my walks I recall walking past this room and each time when I glanced inside there was an elderly being screaming similarly to the exorcist. No matter how scary the image was, I looked in each time as I passed by.

For my second night in the hospital my sister stayed with me. She and my dad forced my mom to go home as she hadn't slept or showered since we had arrived at the hospital. My mom went kicking and screaming but she went. And boy was it good she did as my sister was in for a surprise and a hell of a night. On this night a different nurse came into my room and said it was time to remove the tube from my lungs. Before doing so, he told me to grab a few tissues as there was a tendency for fluid to come out of your opposite nostril, mouth and even eyes during the process. Really? That's pretty gross.

So there I was lying back as the nurse proceeded to pull this tube out of my nose. Inch by inch, foot by foot you can't help but stare intently as this thing exits from within. Directly in front of my nose, I'm sure I was rendered cross eyed as it happened. The nurse, standing in front of me was leaning over my bed slightly. All the while, through the space between his arm and body I could see my sister watching with this semi grossed out look on her face. You could tell she was getting repulsed but she couldn't turn away. I guess we are related. Have you ever been there? Looking at something so nasty yet you can't help but watch? She was fixated. As the tube got closer to the surface, my whole face began to depressurize.

It was the craziest sensation. Not only could you feel it, but it was making noise and more than anything, I think that was freaking my sister out. Yet her face continued to look more intrigued as we proceeded. Then it happened. POP! The tube was out and with it came this brown guck pouring out of my nose, eyes and mouth. It was disgusting! There I was scrambling to grab more tissues. I snatched a few just as another surge of guck made its debut. As I did, I glanced at my sister and she was in the corner with one leg up in the air while simultaneously using her arm to sort of cover her face. She was hiding in disgust yet she never took her eyes off of me. If what she was watching appeared as crazy as her face, I can only imagine how I looked. Where was Instagram when I needed it?

I actually felt bad for my sister that evening as the adventure had just begun. Now everyone that truly knows me knows I'm very particular to say the least when it comes to hygiene and spatial awareness. That night however, all good manners were out the window and I kept her awake constantly with my coughing up phlegm as once your tubes come out of your lungs you simply can't help yourself. It's pretty violent actually. There I was holding on to my belly for dear life so I wouldn't pop my staples and stitches, coughing up the heaviest nastiest phlegm in existence into a paper cup. I've never seen anything like it before or since. Every time the phlegm would hit the bottom of that cup it would do so with a resounding thud. Sorry sis.

Once I got through the second night, things progressed rather smoothly and although it took a little effort, my dad, sister and I were able to convince my mom that I'd be alright staying alone the next few nights. The coughing continued but its wrath diminished as did the thickness of my phlegm making it easier to tolerate. Getting myself out of bed simplified with each attempt and soon enough I didn't rely solely on the assistance of the remote control to prop me up. The frequency of my daily walks increased and they became less of a task and more enjoyable. Instead of having to be told it was time for a walk I started taking them on my own. Gone from my walks was the

IV I had used as a crutch only days before. Somehow I felt the more I walked down that hall the faster I would walk out of the hospital.

Alien Inside Me

Having gone under full anesthesia for my laparotomy, I learned that before being allowed to leave the hospital I had to have a full bowel movement. With my metabolism this was beyond an ordinary task. I know this is kind of personal, but at this point we've shared so much we're family. Unfortunately, full anesthesia can turn this usually routine activity into anything but as it literally turns off your bodily functions. There I was in the hospital, and by day three and four I was beyond stir crazy and wanted out. Despite becoming easier with each attempt, I was ok with the fact that sitting up, walking, coughing, you name it, was far from routine at this point. Basically I was just ready to fly the coup. I'm sure my mom will attest to the fact that I've never been able to sit still in my entire life. I was so active as a child that doctors literally wanted to inject me with tranquilizers to slow me down. As an infant, despite having an extension on my crib and a lock on my door, my parents found me in the kitchen playing with the pots and pans in the stove during the middle of the night.

With that little bit of history, it's no wonder that once doctors told me all I had to do to get out of this place was take a shit I couldn't have been happier. I could do that with my eyes closed. Yeah, guess what? Not so fast! Everyday I'd get "the" feeling. "Ooh ooh I gotta go." Everyday, I'd prop myself up, throw my legs over the side of the bed, shuffle into the bathroom and then…NOTHING!!! "Are you kidding me? Is this a cruel joke?" Then on day five that all changed. I lay in my bed and that feeling hit. This was it, I was sure. I went through my routine in order to get myself into my bathroom. There I was on the "throne" offering myself words of encouragement.

C'mon D, you can do it!

Then all of a sudden, this noise came from within me. It was so loud it began to echo off the walls. It was a long ominous unearthly roar. Shit scared the be-jesus out of me!!! Sitting on the toilet I began frantically looking around trying to figure out where the hell that noise was coming from. Was my bathroom possessed by a demon? "Oh shit, that sound is coming from me!" I thought I was trapped in the movie Alien. I figured it was only a matter of moments until that crazy little creature ate its way out of me from the inside. Then without warning, BOOM!!! I farted.

"Are you kidding? That's it? I can't take it anymore. Let me outta here!" As soon as I was able to get myself out of the bathroom I called the nurse and told her I had a bowl movement. One way or another, I was breaking out of this joint. We called my dad and he came to get me. I was free! I couldn't wait for a real meal. As soon as I got home my dad and I made the biggest BLTs you've ever seen. Guess what? Twenty minutes later that whole bowel movement situation was taken care of.

It was great to be home, however, during my stay in the hospital the anxiety continued to build as we waited for my results. The WAITING… As I've mentioned, this might possibly be one of the more mind wrecking parts of the process. You're already in a place where you can't do anything about your circumstances and you're willing to accept them but the suspense of not knowing what's next is truly mentally tough. Even when you're fortunate to put your mind elsewhere someone would bring it up. It wasn't that anyone was trying to add to the stress of the situation, we just couldn't take not knowing. During times like this when I found myself alone or trying to fall asleep I was left to my thoughts.

Pillow Talk

I have a tendency to keep to myself and when I was sick that was definitely the case. In retrospect, I feel bad for my folks because they would typically ask how I was feeling and more often than not they got treated with one of my favorite one word answers like fine or okay. Truthfully, I did almost all my talking alone in my room both at home and in the hospital when it was time for bed. All the answers my mom continuously sought spilled out onto my pillow each night as I would often talk to my folks behind my closed door as I lay there staring at the ceiling in the dark. Truthfully, during those moments, I talked to just about anyone "out there" that would listen. If only my pillow could have talked…

Hey Ma, hey Pop.

I hope you guys are hanging in there.

I know things are pretty bad right now and I'm sorry.

I'm so sorry for getting sick!

Please know I didn't do it on purpose.

I'm trying my best to stay strong like you've always taught me but it's getting pretty tough.

I know I joked around about getting my Joy Juice, but it's the worst!

Mom, Pop, I really hate throwing up.

I truly despise it!

When this is over I'm never throwing up again!

I'm sorry for complaining but I just don't know who else to talk to.

I know you've always taught me that no matter how bad we have it somebody has it worse and I know that's true but I'm just tired.

I'm really, really, tired!

Mom, Pop… if I die, I want you to know how much I love you.

I love you guys so much!

There I go again…

Sorry for getting so emotional, but if I die I'm really going to miss you guys.

Please tell Jen I love her and that I'm sorry for pouring that container of orange juice over her head when I was little.

While I'm at it Jen, sorry for hitting you with my wiffle ball bat and breaking your nose way back when.

That one truly was an accident.

We've had some great times sis, and you've been the best big sister I could have asked for even though every time we drove through a tunnel you used to tell me a giant octopus was going break through the wall and get me.

Damn, I don't want to die!

Thank you guys so much for being here with me.

I couldn't have gotten this far without you.

Ah man… I knew this wasn't going to be easy, but I didn't know it was going to be this difficult either.

Dear God, I don't know if you've been listening, but I could really use some help right now. I know you probably have more important things on your plate but I hope you can hear me. What did I ever do wrong? I never hurt anybody and I know this is selfish, but why me? You let people go around murdering others and they live to be 100 and I get sick. I really don't understand your logic right now.

You listening?

I don't wanna die God.

Are you listening???

Well if not, Fuck You!

Fuck you for letting me get sick in the first place!

I mean…Alright alright, I'm sorry. I didn't mean it but this is some bull shit. I can take whatever you want to dish out but leave my folks out of this. You're killing them God! What kind of shit is that? It's one thing to put me through it but why them? They're doing all they can to be strong but I can see it on their faces. I even hear them crying sometimes. You really have a sick sense of humor. They're the greatest parents I could ask for and you're torturing them!

I don't know what to say right now God. I'll make a difference one day, you'll see. Just give me a chance.

I CAN DO IT…

I can do it…

I can do it…

These pillow talks practically occurred nightly. I did keep to myself throughout my process and even though I talked to the ceiling, the wall, out the window or into my pillow, the fact remained that no matter how strong or tough I tried to be, I had to get it out. I know all of what I said each night was exactly the type of emotion my mom would have given her left arm to share with me but I simply wasn't capable of sharing it at the time and I'm sorry for that.

Post Op

My Pillow Talk moments were probably the most intense when I stayed alone in the hospital following my laparotomy. Despite being armed with a stainless steel midsection similar to that of a superhero courtesy of the staples adorning my abdomen, they did nothing to protect myself or my family as we were possibly at our most fragile juncture. In the interim, my focus turned to coping and overcoming my new limited mobility. Complementing the impressive looking wound, the amount of internal cutting Dr. Clarke had performed was quite intensive. Trying to sit, stand or walk required special attention to detail as I constantly had to hold a towel to my midsection which in general served as support. However, the primary function of that towel was it gave me something to hold on to, with which to hold my stomach down thus preventing it from expanding when I would cough which was an often occurrence as a result of the anesthesia. My lungs had already been severely damaged from chemo so they took extra long to recuperate following my laparotomy.

When coughing would ensue it was actually quite violent and painful. It was a catch 22 as I was caught between the need of expelling the phlegm in my lungs and the pain of feeling like each time I coughed I was going to tear my staples and stitches. At times I would keel over as I attempted to hold my stomach intact while coughing up a disgusting dark mustard green substance. Somehow it seemed like no matter what I did mustard kept finding its way into my life. Mustard had caused my most vicious moments during chemo and once again it was doing the same.

My having to relearn such basic functions as sitting, standing, walking and even sleeping was all consuming and consequently kept my mind occupied. My folks on the other hand weren't so lucky. As stubborn and determined as I was, they helped me every chance I would allow. However, both my mom and dad were fully consumed by their thoughts of the next steps awaiting us. When I had first gotten diagnosed we had been given good odds yet somehow we found ourselves in the most unexpected predicaments. Following what was supposed to be my final CAT scan, the likelihood of not needing a bone marrow transplant and that this was all some sort of mistake was a mere five percent.

My parents now had to deal with the stress of waiting for my results, the thoughts of my upcoming procedure and treatment combined with the mystery of figuring out how to afford it. How to afford it? Since insurance companies didn't cover it at the time, it was basically a cash only option and the hospital wanted a hefty down payment to get started and proof that you could pay the balance. So much for the Hippocratic Oath. Not knowing what else to do, my mom began trying to devise a way to get on a TV show to plead her case and ask for help. In between calls to everyone she knew that could potentially help make that happen, she began taking my CAT scans to multiple doctors asking for additional opinions.

My folks were in complete disbelief. Getting through our first nine months had taken about all their strength. They were elated when those nine months were complete. Truth was, they were probably happier than me as I was so dilapidated at the end of my treatment I didn't have the energy to celebrate. For them it meant we could all get our lives back and they could watch me once again grow into the healthy son they missed so. Then on that one day with that one phone call all those thoughts of promise were stripped away as fast as they had arrived.

Now they awaited another phone call. One that would detail the new road that awaited us and confirm that somehow, I was sicker than ever. Every other time we had to wait for news it seemed to take a couple of weeks. I didn't know if my parents would be able to hold it together for that long this time around. Fortunately they didn't have to and some news was best delivered in person. Four days after my laparotomy, Dr. Brower came into our room to tell us that I didn't need a bone marrow transplant and I was going to be okay. My parents hugged him as if he was a family member they hadn't seen in years. They began to cry and have a conversation. Funny, when we first met Dr. Brower and I sat in his office as he delivered our fate, the three of them had a conversation as if I wasn't even there. Now as they had done once before they were having a moment all to themselves as if I were invisible. It was still difficult for me to sit up and get out of bed so I was sitting there like "Hello??? I'm over here." When they reemerged my parents embraced and Dr. Brower walked over to my bed. Teary eyed he gave me a hug and told me "We did it!" He was my doctor, my captain, but most of all my friend and we had done it together. We shook hands and looked at each other in the eyes as if to recognize the road we had just traveled.

Thank you, doc!

No, thank you!

I had learned so much from him about how to treat and care for a human being. While some doctors make you feel like a statistic he made me feel like one of his sons. Why then was he thanking me? When I visited his office for a checkup shortly after that day, I had to ask.

Doc, why did you thank me that day in the hospital?

Danny, you've taught me more about handling a difficult situation with grace then I could have ever imagined.

You're a special young man and I'm honored to be your doctor.

Wow! I was speechless. He had saved my life and he was honored?

Going back to my hospital room, as Doctor Brower left my bedside after delivering the good news my parents rushed over to greet me. Before Dr. Brower left, they shook hands and hugged him one more time. Then they practically tackled me. They were so elated. We were all crying and with them on top of me air became scarce.

I can't breathe!!!

They both got up and we all started laughing. Laughing! There was a twist. We hadn't shared a laugh in quite some time. Doing so, just one day prior seemed practically impossible. Just when our options appeared as limited as our chances, relief came in the form of two words.

Phantom Cells

Phantom cells. These are two words that prior to Dr. Brower reciting them that day in my room, myself or my folks had never heard before. Then again, our journey forced us to learn a lot of new words. What made these so special? Phantom Cells. These two words were perhaps the two greatest gifts my family and I were ever given. In a way, you could say I owe my life to these two words. You see, when chemotherapy attacks your body it does so with malicious intent. Everything in its path is public enemy number one. That doesn't always bode well and causes you to have some of your worst days but with chemo you have no choice but to take the good with the bad. As my treatment progressed I took periodic CAT scans and with each one it showed my body reacted favorably and the continual shrinking of my cancer cells.

Remember, Hodgkin's is a form of lymphoma which causes your lymph glands to swell. Consequently, in addition to ridding your glands of the cancer which causes them to swell, chemo is also charged with the task of reducing them down to their normal size. Scan after scan they continued to shrink until that one day upon taking my final CAT scan they had increased greater in size than the day I first met Dr. Brower. How could this be? Using track and field as an analogy, this was the same as having a huge lead at the 300 meter mark only to have that infamous monkey which I'll talk about later, jump on your back and you finish dead last. What had gone so drastically wrong between the sixth and ninth month? It was chemotherapy's wrath. It was so destructive that it literally obliterated my cancer cells, leaving their remains everywhere. Dr. Brower compared it to the blowing up of a balloon. He said "Imagine you blow up a balloon and let all the air out yet the balloon keeps its inflated shape. That's what happened to your cancer cells."

Let the air out of a balloon yet it keeps it shape? What exactly was he saying? Well, my cancer cells were the empty balloons that held their shape and there was nothing in them. No cancer. Nada. In actuality I was okay and I didn't need a bone marrow transplant. Was he kidding? Remember, a couple weeks before my dad had asked what the odds were that my CAT scan was wrong and Dr. Brower had told us a mere five percent. He wasn't kidding. Till this day, if I have a CAT scan and the doctor responsible for reading it is unfamiliar with my medical background they would think I have cancer. Despite destroying them, chemo essentially blew up my cancer cells yet they give the image of being alive and well. Phantom cells. We had never heard of them but who were we to argue?

That few weeks of our journey provided us with the most extreme emotional mind fuck. True to form of any tormentor it tangled hope in front of us only to take it away and then give it back to us. When I received and finished my last injection I looked like a walking corpse. I needed help doing just about everything. As I mentioned, I might have been too tired to celebrate, but knowing on that day that there were no more injections was absolutely thrilling. My all day long confessions, my gout, phlebitis, loss of hair, pimples, dry skin, dehydration, migraines, sensitivity to light, low white blood count constantly causing some form of infection, brittle bones, taking pills, and my pillow talk all of which I so despised cancer and chemo for forcing me to do had finally come to an end. At last I could reclaim my life. Seemingly overnight, that all changed with that one phone call. The process had been such an emotional strain that the thought of repeating it was too great. At least until Dr. Brower explained the alternative. Then two words entered my life and vocabulary and changed all that. Phantom cells. Honestly, I didn't give a fuck what they were as long as they meant we didn't have to repeat the road we had just traveled.

Remission/College/Getting Back in Shape

With the benefit of good news on our side I officially started remission and soon enough, college. It took about four weeks after my laparotomy for me to regain enough stability and confidence to start attending class at Queens College. I was still void of the basic energy to make it through a full day but it was great to begin my slow return towards being a teenager again. Emotionally that meant a great deal as my world essentially had come to a halt while every friend I had progressed and went off to college. With all my friends gone, it felt like starting all over.

Some things remained the same as despite having closed the chapter on my chemo I still had to carry a thermos full of water everywhere I went to combat dehydration. I refilled that thing at least ten times a day. I guess all of my friends hadn't left. I still looked sick and many of my chemo inspired friends kept me company for a good part of that first year. My I.D. picture from Queens College tells the story of a time long since past. I took very few photos when I was sick as I hated the image they represented. Anytime I'd look at them I couldn't believe what I was seeing. Even when I saw one recently I asked my mom how they let me out of the house looking like that. She replied, "What were we supposed to do, we thought you might be dying."

Gradually however, one by one new signs of life began to reappear throughout the better part of that first year. Despite the discoloration of my veins remaining for quite some time, about half way through the year I could finally straighten and flex my arms without pain or assistance. Speaking of discomfort, the extreme pain and the gout that caused it, found its exit as well and they took with it those huge dissolvable pills I had to take to combat it. Perhaps greatest of all, that wispy head of nothingness that I had come to know as a head of hair gradually got replaced by a thick head of curls I had missed so. Once they grew back, similar to Sampson I never wanted to cut them again. Armed with the strength of my fro I defiantly put my fist in the air declaring "Never again!" I had no intention of ever reliving my journey.

No longer on Prednisone, the thousands of pimples that had adorned my neck, shoulders and back and the embarrassment and disgust that came with them dissipated. The Prednisone induced weight I had gained was still there but at least the constant bloatedness went away and I didn't have to gag anymore when I took those pills. Once again I could feel better and more confident about myself. Remission? This was one new word I didn't mind learning. Remission was restoring order but lost forever was that olive brown complexion of mine that I had loved so but I've learned to accept that as clearly it's better than the alternative.

In all, I attended Queens College for two years. It wasn't until the second year however, that I actually had the energy to socialize and start making friends, some of whom remain close to this day. It was also in that second year of Queens College that I began an attempt at getting back in shape as I dreamed of going away to school and playing sports. Prior to getting sick I rowed for one of New York's premier rowing clubs. I was the youngster of the team but I had always remembered one guy from our training above all the rest. Chuck.

It seemed no matter when I went to the boat house he was there training. I knew I wanted to get back into shape but I'd be lost trying to do so on my own. I found the team phone list from two years earlier and took a shot.

Hello?

Is Chuck there please?

This is he.

Hi, I don't know if you remember me, but this is Danny Alotta.

I was the youngest rower on the team a couple of years ago when I got sick.

He remembered. According to him "Of course" he remembered. While I was sick the squad had gotten me a team jacket and bag. After we exchanged pleasantries, I explained that I wanted to get back in shape and that I always recalled him being at the boathouse working out and wondered if I could train with him. He obliged and with that he began coaching and training me. I was in horrific shape physically. During my treatment, one of my lungs collapsed and I often had to use a little breathing gizmo with a ball inside to strengthen my lungs. Doing sprints, ladders or weight circuits were completely out of the question.

We started slow. It felt the same as learning how to walk again and that's exactly how we started, with long walks. When I finally hit the rowing machine (erg), Chuck told me not to worry about my time. Simply focus on form and everything else would follow. However, everyone that has ever rowed or sat on an erg knows that the 500M split time means everything. I had been instructed to perform the equivalent of a paddle but that split time on the display kept staring at me daring me to give it a whirl. The wheel on an ergometer makes a noticeable sound when it spins but it recites and unmistakable roar when someone cranks away and hammers down on the footboard. That growl in a boat house or training facility can cause heads to spin trying to figure out who was on the other end of the statement. I wanted to reclaim that feeling, to have the machine hum beneath me. I gradually increased my paddle to a trot and from a trot to an all out sprint which by the fourth stroke of that outburst it was over and I was left to catch my breath. Damn, this was going to be more difficult than I thought. It took several minutes to slow my sporadic breathing and regain my composure. When I did, I returned to my instructed paddle. Lesson learned.

From that day forward we methodically developed muscles I had lost and increased my lung capacity. Chuck has always been the smartest training partner I've ever had. In all the years I have known him he has averaged approximately one world championship victory per year. Over the course of the year we worked together I shed all of those extra pounds and returned to my pre chemo weight of 140. It was an incredible feeling returning to a visually looking athletic form that had been stripped away from me after the first five days of my treatment. By the time the following fall arrived not only had my weight normalized, I was able to compete for a seat (the equivalent of a starting spot) on the rowing team upon arrival at Temple University.

Temple University

Getting the chance to go away to Temple University was the best experience of my life. Essentially it gave me the chance to separate myself from my old life and start anew as it wasn't until I had the opportunity to go to TU that I truly felt like I got my life back. When I arrived there, I essentially still had no social life, had yet to officially return to competitive sports and most of all had yet to return to being a carefree adolescent. It was the greatest place I could have dreamed of spending my college days. So great in fact I never wanted to leave and I stayed for undergrad and two graduate degrees. When the conclusion of undergrad approached I couldn't imagine leaving so I spoke with my mentor about my options. He asked if I had ever thought about grad school. My dad had always told me if I ever went to grad school I should get an MBA in Finance. There it was. I promptly took the GMAT and enrolled in Temple's business school the following fall. While in B-school the tech world caught fire and a handful of schools including Temple created E-Business programs which I would enroll in and receive an additional degree. When all was said and done I had my BS, MBA & MS and those three degrees were complemented by three sport programs.

When I arrived at Temple I was nearly 6' 1" and 140 pounds. Despite being tremendously stronger than I had been, I was still quite weak. Following my first year I decided to attend summer school. I asked the strength coach if I could workout with him to get stronger and he told me that the football team would be working out during the summer and I was more than welcome to join them. I accepted.

By the end of the summer I had impressed my coach with my work ethic and learned to love a sport I had never played on an organized level. Not to mention I gained strength I was previously unaware I possessed. As the summer crept towards its completion my strength coached ask me if I had ever thought about playing for the team and that he could arrange to have me walk on. Intrigued, I decided I wanted to play. First however I would have to tell my mom.

My mom hated football and when I was a child she told me I could play any sport I'd like except football, to which I obliged. When I started playing hockey she couldn't believe the ailments I continuously came home with but what could she say, I had listened to her and it wasn't football. During that first summer at Temple when I mentioned to my dad that I had planned on walking onto the football team, his immediate response was "You're going to have to talk to you mom."

There we sat at the kitchen table. My dad helped me out and started us off.

Your son has something he needs to tell you.

I took a deep breath trying to figure out how to say it. Just as I was about to my mom interrupted.

Did you get your girlfriend pregnant?

Wow, that was easier than I thought it was going to be.

A little background on myself; I'm somewhat of a smartass and I couldn't resist going with the flow of the moment.

Daniel Philip Alotta!

Uh Oh, there goes my full government again.

I taught you better than this.

I taught you to use condoms.

I did, it wasn't my fault.

The condom broke.

My mom was fuming. I needed a way out.

Okay okay, I'm just joking.

I have decided to play football though.

Football?

I wish you could have seen her face. She had this perplexed look that was priceless.

What are you talking about?

I'm going to play football at school.

Flag football?

No football, football. On the actual team at school.

I kid you not, that's when she cried. She balled out! When she thought I had gotten my girlfriend pregnant she was mad but no tears. When she realized I was seriously going to play football at Temple it was over.

What are you talking about?

How could you do this?

You're going to get hurt!

Have you checked with Dr. Brower?

What position are you going to play?

She asked me so many questions I couldn't think straight. When I told her I planned on playing wide receiver she immediately called my cousins who were sports fanatics to find out exactly what a wide receiver did and how much they got hit. She was not too pleased.

Nevertheless, that fall I joined the football team as a walk on. It was probably the best athletic decision I have ever made. Admittingly, in the grand scheme of things I was a horrible football player. I didn't understand the language, the formations and I didn't like getting hit but I was enamored with the camaraderie and the physical tasks I was now capable of. Because I was so skinny when I started training with the team the strength coached worked with me each morning in the weight room. Within a few months I began lifting weights that I previously thought unimaginable. Despite not being overly fond of the hitting drills I loved the fact that I emerged from them unscathed each time. Every time I got hit and got up it gave me a rush of adrenaline knowing that once again I was strong. By doing so, football did for me what nothing else had up until that point. It restored my confidence in full. That swagger and invincibility that I had lost years before was back. Even after I decided a couple years later that football wasn't the type of sport to be played on a whim, I continued to train with the guys every chance I got. During summer workouts one day, one of the guys who had gone on to the league asked me "Do you ever miss a workout?" I explained my medical history and that sports and staying in shape was a contributing factor to me still being here. Having no idea, he was shocked. I know he and a handful of other players wondered why I had even tried my hand at the sport but you could see in his eye that day, he understood.

Following that first fall season playing football I transitioned back into rowing shape which was vastly different. Instead of being conditioned for quick three or four second spurts I now had to regain my endurance. But hey, I was invincible again remember. I was stronger and faster than ever. There was nothing I couldn't do and nothing that could faze me. Then I woke up one day that spring semester and that all changed.

Like every other day I had gotten up and gone to practice. Life was grand. Upon getting back to my dorm I jumped in the shower so I could change and head to class. There I stood water beating down when I noticed I had what looked like two golf balls protruding from my groin area. Damn! I fell to the floor of the shower and put my hands over my face. Throughout the course of my treatment I had become keenly aware of my body, especially my glands. Keep in mind Hodgkin's is a type of lymphoma that affects your lymph glands which we have throughout our body. There were a couple key areas that Dr. Brower always checked and told me to pay attention to. The first being my arm pits and the second being my groin. When I originally got diagnosed I had never even noticed swollen glands. Quite possibly at that point I didn't know what to look for, but on this day I did and they were huge.

I sat there on the floor of the shower for nearly an hour. I never made it class. How could this be? I was lost. I walked around campus aimlessly that day. There had to be a mistake. Hadn't my glands gotten the message that I was invincible again? I kept walking around campus until it was time to return to practice that afternoon. Practice, that's it! That would make everything better, right? After all, it had restored me back to who I once was and better. It was the ultimate source of my invincibility. It worked. I went to practice that day and killed it. See, I knew what I was talking about. All I had to do was keep going to practice and I'd be okay. That night when I took a shower my glands proved my theory right. They were not nearly as swollen as they were that morning. I felt great. I was a genius. Not that I told my friends what had happened that day but we partied anyway. It was college. We partied just because it was Tuesday.

The next morning I got up and returned to the source of my strength. All was well and practice was terrific. Upon looking down at my groin when I got in the shower, my two friends from the previous day had returned and they must have brought a few associates with them because they were even bigger. It was nothing I told myself. It had to be nothing. I went to class. Midway through, I started feeling off. By my second class I was dragging my feet. It was early spring and it wasn't hot but I was sweating. I walked myself over to health services to see Dr. Johnston. She knew my medical background and had always told me if I needed anything not to worry about making an appointment just come straight away.

She instantly knew something was wrong. We had seen each other the previous Friday as I had started getting a cold and she gave me an antibiotic to knock it out of my system. Clearly it hadn't worked. Once she looked at my glands she knew what we were dealing with was no ordinary cold.

Danny, you have to call your doctor.

Are you sure?

I just have cold.

I have a bad cold.

Danny, are you listening to me?

You have to call your doctor.

I had heard Dr. Johnston but it didn't register. There had to be a mistake. All I had to do was give it a day or two and I'd be fine. She'd see. I'd show them all. The following day I woke up with a fever of 102. In disbelief I decided to ride it out. Somehow this would rectify itself. It had to. Hadn't everyone gotten the message that I had returned to form. Yes I had been sick, but now I had gone away to school and I hadn't looked back. It was time to reclaim my life. That Friday when I woke my fever had gone up to 103.5. I could barely get out of bed. I did have to call Dr. Brower.

I picked up the phone and began to dial. Before I finished, I hung up. I sat back on my bed and began to cry. How could this be happening? I had finally been given a second chance. It just didn't seem to make sense. It was a few hours before I found the courage again to place that call. As it rang, my heart began to pound. Laura answered. Wouldn't you know it Dr. Brower had just left for vacation. Laura said she was getting ready to do the same, told me when they'd return and gave me the number for the covering doctor. Then she asked me a question I hadn't anticipated.

Danny, have you called your parents?

FUCK, my parents! How was I going to tell them? I couldn't. This was a phone call they'd never expect. I always called to say hello but this? This would destroy them. They had been tortured watching me be sick. The thought of a reoccurrence would absolutely shatter their world. This phone call would be way out of left field. Maybe somehow I could sneak back to New York, go to the doctor, find out this was all a mistake and return to school? That was an idea. I could do it. Yeah right, imagine that.

I needed a day to gather myself. Perhaps I could sleep this off and by the next morning everything would be better. Night came and went and when I awoke my fever had crept up to 104 and my glands had swelled further. I had traveled this road before. With hindsight now on my side, I was keenly aware of the signs. As I mentioned, with every physical examination Dr. Brower had always taught me to be particularly conscious of my glands. It was part of the process of taking charge of your health.

Remission. As defined by the dictionary (freedictionary.com), remission is the "subsiding of the symptoms of disease." They may have subsided, but I never forgot them. With a high fever and extremely swollen glands, I was all too clear on what this meant.

A million thoughts raced through my head. Since arriving at Temple I had gotten my life back. All those days of lying on the couch and going to the doctor were in my past. I refused to even think about them. They didn't exist to me anymore. I had left my nemesis behind and replaced them with friends, girlfriends, teammates, parties you name it. This was my chance to make up for lost time. How could I go back? How could I take my parents back? I thought about the day they dropped me off at Temple. It was a proud day. A day they had thought may never come. But it had come. Collectively it was our new beginning. Now I lay in bed pondering how to strip that all away. I had always wondered how my mom found the strength to call my dad time and again to deliver similar news. Faced with the same task I began to rehearse my words in preparation for that call. Had my mom done the same? Did she have to build up the courage the same as I was now trying to do? When I finally found the nerve, I propped myself up in my bed. My heart began to race and my hands shook. Was this what it was like? Was this what my mom felt each time? I took a deep breath. I was ready. The phone was ringing.

Hello?

Hey Ma.

What's the matter?

You don't sound so good.

I have a pretty bad cold.

Despite preparing myself for the call I still didn't know how to break the news. Since the day I had gotten sick, any time I had a cold or dare to sneeze, my mom always got a little nervous.

Did you go to the doctor?

You probably need an antibiotic.

You're pushing yourself too hard.

Ma, I went to the doctor and she gave me medicine.

But my fever is 104 and…

Just as I had built up the courage to tell her, 104 was all she could hear. She stopped me dead in my tracks.

104! How long have…

MA!!!

I had her attention.

I spoke with Laura yesterday, Dr. Brower's on vacation but she gave me the number for his covering physician.

You spoke with Laura?

Dr. Brower?

Why did you call…

MA!!!

Reluctantly she paused but her breathing intensified.

I'm so sorry ma!

I'm so sorry!

With that tears began to fall down my cheek.

Danny, why are you sorry?

What are you sorry about?

I have to come home.

Danny what's wrong?

It's my glands ma.

They're really swollen.

I mean really swollen!

There was dead silence on the other end. I could hear the muffled sound of my mom crying. This wasn't the phone call she had expected. In the background there was the sound of paper crumbling. It sounded as if she was trying with all her might to squeeze every ounce of emotion into that paper as if somehow, she would manage to squeeze hard enough to make all of this go away. She still hadn't said a word though.

Ma?

Yes.

Are you there?

Yes sweetheart, I'm here.

She was still crying and so was I. Despite the fact that we were on the on the phone, somehow I think she had needed a minute alone to process what I had said. It just so happens she took it right then.

Hello?

You did hear me right?

Yes dear.

Now please start over and tell me everything.

Indeed she had taken a moment. Regrouped and focused, I had her attention. We spent the next several minutes talking in detail about what was going on. Her questioning was meticulous as she covered every detail. There was no way I was going to manage one word answers here. Once satisfied with my responses the conversation concluded. My folks arrived at my dorm a few hours later.

Despite talking to me earlier that morning and knowing I wasn't well, when they walked into my room after being signed into the dorm by my roommate, it was a sight they hadn't expected. Prior to this visit, every other occasion they had made the trip to Philly was for a good reason be it a race or simply to say hello and take me to dinner. On this day I lay there in my bed with barely enough energy to greet them. Both my fever and glands were thriving. When I looked up and saw their faces, their eyes closed and their heads fell. It was a sight they had never expected to see again. My dad walked over and sat on the bed next to me as my mom retreated to the bathroom. The scene was too much. She needed to escape.

Hey kid.

How you feeling?

Not too good, Pop.

It was a rare occurrence for me to say anything but fine. There was no point pretending.

I know son.

We're going to take you home and figure this all out.

At that moment, my mom walked back into the room. She had clearly been crying but had managed to gather herself. She sat at the end of my bed and the three of us talked briefly. Forever the mom, she placed her hand on my forehead to check on my fever.

You're burning up.

We have to get you home.

They helped me out of bed. I showed them my glands to which they were amazed. Even the skin on my torso was hot and red in color. We gathered a few of my things and we were off. I couldn't even tell you about the car ride home as I slept the entire way. It was a couple weeks before spring break.

That Monday we met with Dr. Brower's covering physician. He was a nice guy, but Dr. Brower was my dude. Guess I was partial. It didn't take long into the examination for him to express the gravity of the situation. Within minutes he retrieved my mom and told her we needed an immediate biopsy. Naturally we called Dr. Clarke. Wouldn't you know it he was on vacation as well? What was this national doctor vacation week?

Instead we met with his covering physician as well. She was a splendid person who I liked instantly. She was to be in surgery the following day but saw us the day after despite a full schedule. She spoke with my mom and me and then she and I went into the examination room. She had already been fully briefed on my medical history so once she saw my glands she decided it was best to do the biopsy right then in order to save time providing I didn't have any objection. Naturally I did not.

Based upon her experience she anticipated the whole thing taking about twenty minutes. I leaned back; she cleaned the area of interest and then gave me an injection of that "good stuff." Within moments I was numb. With that she took her scalpel and made the first incision. The skin in my groin peeled open like nothing I had ever seen. I'm not exactly sure why but I have always been fascinated by this sort of thing. Instead of lying back completely with my eyes closed, I remained upright enough so that I could watch the entire process. She was shocked.

You sure you don't want to lay back and close your eyes?

Oh no, I want to watch.

Really?

Can I help?

Can I make an incision?

Uhhhhh no!

I think she wanted to ask me if I was out of my mind but she was nice about it.

I tell you what.

Here's a gauze pad.

When I need you to, I'll tell you when to gently wipe the blood away.

How's that?

Does that work for you?

That's great!

She made me put on surgical gloves. It was so official like. There I was, assistant to my very own surgery. How cool was that? Later when I told my folks and sister they all thought I was crazy.

My doctor proceeded to snip away. As I intently peeked inside the opening, I saw the gland she was targeting. Truthfully, I wasn't so impressed. Prior to being peeled back and revealed it had looked like a massive golf ball protruding from inside me. Now that I was staring face to face with my gland it resembled the shape of a small bean more than anything. Each time she tried to separate it from inside me it seemed to move. Perfectly fine with me, there was a lot of blood which meant the more I got to help. It started bleeding to the point where she was forced to use a little clamp in order to stop it. Who needed the Discovery channel? Time continued to pass and the initial anesthesia began to wear off. She had to readminister it two additional times. By the time we were finished about 75 minutes had passed. She sewed me up which might have been one of the coolest parts of the entire process. I rejoined my mom at which point the doctor came out to say all had gone well and we'd have the results as soon as possible.

Being as though we were near Central Park and it was a beautiful spring day, my mom and I got ice cream and sat on a park bench for a while. Central Park is my favorite place in the city and relaxing there in the sun allowed time and circumstance to stand still. When we were ready to get going I couldn't bring myself to head home so I left my mom and walked around the city for a while. There wasn't much she could say to deter me as I'm quite stubborn. Despite being downtown, I even visited my dad at his restaurant just to say hey. After a few hours, the area surrounding the wound began tightening up so I went home. Later that evening, when my dad returned from work I was asleep and as you guessed, on the couch. I looked up at him as he walked in.

You look like shit.

It hurts doesn't it?

My dad has always been a straight to the point kind of guy. Not to mention that he warned me walking around all afternoon might aggravate the incision. When he got home, I was pale as a ghost and it hurt like hell. Let this serve as a word to the wise. Everything I had watched earlier that day I could now feel. It was as if the visuals from that morning accentuated the pain that evening. I'm not sure if that's the norm but if you ever find yourself with the option of closing your eyes or watching a procedure, I'd probably say you're better off closing your eyes.

I was much better when I woke up the next day. It was a good thing as we were scheduled for a new sort of CAT scan as this one was radioactive. Apparently they had to inject me with some sort of radioactive fluid which I believe made my insides glow even greater than the iodine, when the machine took its images. Prior to getting the injection they informed me that I wasn't allowed to hug or be around children or pregnant women for several days. Not that I made a habit of hanging out with either, but with a warning like that I wasn't sure I wanted the injection. Want or not the scan went on as scheduled and true to form I slept through it. With the all too familiar road of waiting for results upon us my mom went bananas day after day as they never came. The following Monday when Dr. Brower returned he got up to speed on the events of the week. Once he found out everything he had me come for a visit the next day.

Hey Dr. Brower.

How are you feeling?

I've been better but I've definitely been worse.

My fever is better so basically, I'm fine doc.

Just a little confused that's all.

Not that I don't like coming to see you, I just didn't expect this.

Me neither Danny but we're going to sort it out.

Do I need chemo again?

We don't know for sure.

Based upon all the notes from my colleague, it looks that way but it's too soon to say.

If we do Dr. Brower, I'm not leaving Temple.

I'll just commute home for my injections.

If we get that far we can always make arrangements for you in Philly if you'd like?

No sir Dr. Brower, you're the only one I'd trust.

We talked for a little bit longer. Like Robin Williams in "The Dead Poet Society," he was my leader. Just as Ethan Hawke did in the movie, I was ready to stand up on a desk and declare "Oh Captain

My Captain." There was no else that could steer this ship out of the murky waters we were facing. We had learned a great deal from each other over the course of the five years we had known one another. If there was a battle to be had we were going into it together as we had done before. We agreed, shook hands and joined my folks in his office where he gave them the low down. By this point my mom was pulling her hair out in anticipation of our results. He told us that the lab was doing a really thorough job cross referencing them to all my previous specimens. That was great and all but it did nothing to calm her nerves.

Nevertheless we went home and that all too familiar scene of my mom jumping out of her seat each time the phone rang ensued. After two more days I couldn't take it anymore. I had to regain my sanity. Nearly two weeks from the day I had left school I showed up at morning practice. My teammates and especially my coach looked stunned.

What are you doing here?
It's time for practice isn't it?
Have you been cleared for practice?
I cleared myself.
Danny you can't be here.
I'm not leaving coach.
I need this.
I need to get my mind right.
I need to prove to myself I'm ok.

We stared at each other. I extended my hand and he did the same. We shook hands and with that I joined my teammates and started practice. While I was doing box jumps, which are exactly what they sound like, my stitches became none too pleased and a few spots of blood dripped down my leg. When my coached noticed, he ordered me to go to the training room. I denied. I had to finish. It was different this time. This was personal. I had to let myself know I could beat this thing.

Five days after arriving back at school that phone call came.
Hello?

YOU'RE OK!!!
YOU'RE OK!!!
My mom was screaming on the other end of the phone. She kept saying it over and over. I couldn't get a word in to save my life. Then again my life had just been saved.

YOU'RE OK!!!
I LOVE YOU SO MUCH!!!
YOU'RE OK!!!

Finally I was able to break through and my mom explained that my results were perfect. Dr. Brower's best guess to what had caused all this was an allergic reaction to the medicine I had received a few weeks earlier at school. Hence the fever, swollen glands, and red torso. The antibiotic I had been given back at school contained sulfur. I had no previously known allergies so there was no reason to think I would have any other reaction beyond curing the cold I had gotten. Needless to say that was the last time I've taken any medicine containing sulfur. All that fuss. I don't regret it for one moment however, as those three weeks taught me possibly the greatest lesson I've ever learned. From the time I had arrived at Temple, my refusal to look back and respect the road I had traveled to get there caused me to take it for granted. As a result of that eye opener, a day doesn't go by where I don't appreciate simply waking up. The spiritual side of me always figured that was God's way of pulling on my collar and saying "Hey, not so fast! Don't you forget!"

I will admit that believing I was about to be sick again caused me to go off the deep end and party practically every remaining night of that semester. The thought, even for one minute that I was going back down the road that I loathed so caused me to want to have as much fun as possible. There was no reeling me back in. My mentor, friend and teacher Jeffrey Montague called a meeting with me and all of my teachers to discuss my grades which began to drop drastically. They all knew what had just happened but they wanted to know what was going on with me as no one had ever seen me do so poorly on tests. I explained that the recent events made me appreciate living so much that I had planned on partying and party I did. I told it to them straight. I wasn't going to disrespect them by not showing up to class, but I had no intention of opening a book the rest of the semester. Believe it or not, they understood. Once I got it out of my system and that semester was over, I was able to find a balance.

Having an additional scare reinforced that constant fear within me and I believe every other cancer patient that no matter how diligent you are, at any time it could come back. When I first got sick, my mind was still invincible despite my body not being capable of the most basic task. Once I received my diagnosis my mind followed suit as I believed something was wrong with me. As I withered away I knew I could only go out with friends on rare occasions. Chemo defended me against cancer, but if I went out with my friends and something happened where I had to defend myself it rendered me incapable of doing so.

Believing I was sick again strengthened my belief of making the most of my time at Temple. Therefore, when I stopped rowing I joined the track team as the coach and I were friendly. Officially I became a team manager as I was in grad-school hoping to receive a medical redshirt which is when you're allotted extra playing time due to medical hardship. Similar to football, I had never run track before which quickly became evident the first time coach told me to sprint one lap and that infamous monkey climbed on my back at the start of the third turn. Welcome to the 400. For those of you unfamiliar, this monkey can't be found in your local zoo. Instead you can find this imaginary villain at tracks and sporting facilities across the globe as it rears its head typically at a critical juncture of a race or event causing the competitor to fatigue and all but come to a halt. At the end of the day I wasn't the best runner either but I worked as hard as anyone and didn't miss practice. We did everything together and the track team became my family. I wish I had found the sport sooner. Even as I write this book I can't wait for our team reunion at this year's PENN Relays.

Lingering Effects

Cancer. Chemotherapy. Joy Juice. No matter what name I use, one thing remains constant. The effects of my experience resonate through me until this day and I have to believe that will remain throughout the course of my life. First and foremost I absolutely despise throwing up. Truly, I have a hatred for it. So much so I haven't vomited in over eighteen years. It's not that I haven't been sick since and needed to hurl, but I absolutely refuse to. I'll do anything and everything in my power not to. I know we can find another parallel to a "Seinfeld" episode, but then again everyone has always said I need to write a sitcom or two. A little foreshadowing perhaps?

Yes I have a number of lingering effects but we'll get back to them as they go way beyond me. It's so interesting to me how so many years have passed since I was sick yet if my parents and I talk about our journey their emotion remains as raw as ever. Perhaps talking with me about it all these years later my mom is finally capturing the moments I was unable to share back when. My dad on the other hand, even though he doesn't remember all the events with the same detail as my mom, I believe he calculatingly suppresses them. When we have spoken about that time, he has a threshold and once it's crossed, it's over. When talking about it and he reaches that point I usually get his classic response. "Can we change the fuckin' subject?" If you know my dad, that's vintage Phil. The point is, the experience is still fresh for them. It's something they carry with them every day and they'll never be able to let go of it and I lived. Had that not been the case, I honestly can't imagine the baggage they would carry or if they would be able to carry it at all. I have a friend who lost her daughter to cancer and she told me that if it wasn't for her other children she would have killed herself. I talked about this with my dad and he said he completely understood her feelings. As you may have guessed, before our conversation went any further we changed the fuckin' subject.

Despite being a teenager that really didn't understand what was happening when I was diagnosed, it has caused me to appreciate the simplicities and fragility of everyday life to a degree I don't think the average person can comprehend. However, from the day I was well enough to attend Temple University, I have been on a constant quest to make up for that period of time that was stripped from me. It's odd actually. I know technically you can't make up for lost time but somehow deep down I believe it's possible. At times while at school that pursuit led me to go straight to practice after partying all night. To this day, I swear I actually fell asleep and started dreaming while running one morning. Even today, if I'm out late, regardless of what time I go to bed I still wake up early for fear of "missing" the day. I would rather walk around exhausted than have a day and the opportunities that come with each sunrise pass me by.

This quest to replace lost time, has added to my stubbornness causing me to believe that I can do everything only to result in me running myself into the ground. Not to say I don't believe in my capabilities, but trying to do everything at once is a formula for disaster and trying to do so has resulted in some humbling experiences. At times it has caused me to lose focus and consequently taken longer to accomplish certain things in my life as I always believe things will work out in the end as they did before. I have had to learn that having a strong team around me is actually a compliment and an attribute as opposed to a testament that I wasn't capable of handling an entire task on my own.

In my personal relationships I have been extremely blessed to date some incredible women that would have made great lifelong partners. Although, having cancer has made me more sensitive and compassionate towards certain aspects of life. Post chemo and my journey, when I watch movies that strike a chord it's nothing for me to tear up or start crying whereas previously they would have had no effect. In my relationships when my significant other has had an issue or wanted to talk about something that was bothering them, my journey has caused me to become indifferent at times, which when you're in a relationship often doesn't bode well. Things are relative and what one person considers major might not show up on another person's radar which is exactly what happens in my case. Understanding this has been an ongoing process for me thanks to my nemesis and I know I need to do better. That lack of communication I exhibited as a child intensified while I was sick as I didn't want to talk. When a significant other has brought up an issue that I didn't regard as important I often dismissed it and wouldn't talk about it which as you can imagine can be mindboggling to deal with.

Conversely, when I love now, I do so way more intensely. Chemo and cancer taught me that the greatest gift we can share with someone is ourselves and time. I admit maturation plays a part in this as well, but having stared this foe in the eye my appreciation for not only life but those close to me has intensified immensely. If any past girlfriend reads this please know I truly loved you and cherished the time we spent even though at times I was exasperating and seemed aloof or disinterested. Knowing that being in good shape is a major reason why I was able to handle everything, I often made going to the gym a priority over everything else. I know chasing time is a race I can't win as it's the one opponent that never slows down. Unfortunately, the athlete in me has always believed I just have to train a little harder in order to come out victorious. Hopefully, I'll come to terms with this one day.

Cancer. This nemesis of mine has presented me with some interesting challenges. Even the fact that I write about it in the present tense despite technically being cured for quite some time is interesting to me. Officially I have cleared the hurdles cancer threw in front of me. Yet its impact clearly resonates inside me and in my daily actions so how can I address it in the past tense? Chemo attacked both the good and bad within me and as a result, I have to carry lozenges with me everywhere as chemotherapy destroyed my vocal chords. They've recovered greatly but if I have an extended conversation my throat instantly gets sore. If I raise my voice or have to talk over music or noise while I'm out it takes a matter of seconds to feel the effects. How can I speak of this foe completely in the past when its lingering effects are so prevalent? This impact extends to my folks as well. Whether it's the emotion that remains as raw as the day we received my diagnosis or their superstition of not wanting to over recognize our good fortune, they simply want me to continue to be healthy.

They think it's a great achievement and they're extremely proud that I've written a book, screenplay, a one person show and started a foundation that will leverage the power of fashion to do for other sick kids what I did for myself. When I was sick they would often marvel that I would sport my best duds only to sit on the couch or go to the doctor. It worked though and I would feel better about myself. Despite that fact, they prefer not to stir the water and simply be gracious that everything worked out.

"Danny, You're Cured"

I'll never forget the day Dr. Brower gave me the news that I was officially cured. It was almost exactly eleven years to the day he and I had met. We had just finished my check up which at the time I received twice a year. Per the norm, at every visit he always took some notes. On this day however, when he finished he closed my file, lowered his head for a moment, took a deep breath and paused. He had never done that before and I actually thought something was wrong. When he raised his head his eyes were teary. Now I definitely thought something was wrong.

Danny, we've come a long way and it brings me so much pleasure to tell you you're officially cured.

I was stunned. Cured? That was a word that for eleven years seemed to exist in some far off land. When you're sick you pray to hear that word yet you almost don't think it's possible. I know he was my captain, but was he sure? He wasn't going to take it back was he? We had shared jokes before but this couldn't be one could it?

What'd you say Dr. Brower?

Danny, you're cured.

Just as he had taken a deep breath and lowered his head to deliver the news, I now needed to do the same in order to digest it. I truly couldn't believe it, but it was true. When I raised my head the tears that had been in his eyes as he spoke were now flowing out of mine. "Oh Captain, My Captain." As I knew he could, he had led me out of the murky waters that had been all consuming.

We really did it, doc?

We did, Danny.

Crying, I stood up to shake his hand and he put his arms around me.

We did it, Danny!

Thank you, doc!

No, thank you!

I love you, son.

I love you too, Dr. Brower.

When we finished hugging we shook hands and looked into each other's eyes. No words were necessary. Our eye contact was all the acknowledgement we needed. I wasn't his son but he had cared for me as such and I looked up to him in certain respects like I did my own father. He was my captain and best of all, my friend.

As was the routine any time I got a check up, I had to call from the office to let my parents know everything was okay. I was dying to tell them the news but some things you have to say in person. My mom happened to be home and my dad was at work. Combined with the fact that I was already in Manhattan and I didn't think it was fair to make my dad wait all day to learn the news, I decided to jump on the train and head to his restaurant. When I walked out of Dr. Brower's office the reality of the moment hit me and I had to take a seat against the building. I sat there reflecting for about fifteen minutes. I thought about every injection, every pill, my operations, the nights I couldn't sleep because the pain was too great, my parents conversations I had overheard on those sleepless nights, my sister's face that night in the hospital when they took the tubes out of my lungs and every minute that I spent spewing my guts in the bathroom. I hated chemo and on that day with those two words "You're cured," I had finally closed a huge chunk of a painful chapter. **WOW!!!** As soon as I regained my composure I literally ran to the train station because I couldn't wait to share the joy I was feeling.

When I arrived at the restaurant my dad was in his office sitting at his desk.

Hey Pop.

Hey kid.

This is a surprise, what are you doing here?

Guess what?

What?

Dr. Brower told me today that I'm cured!

It's not often in life that a son consoles his father but this was one of those times. Those two words seemed nearly as strong as the kryptonite he had encountered eleven years prior. He covered his eyes and began crying as hysterically as he and I once had the day we called the sperm bank. We walked towards each other and embraced as if we never planned on letting go. Once again this was our moment. Tears were falling on each other's shoulders at an uncontrollable pace.

I love you, son!

I love you too, Pop!

Eventually we came up for air and when we did his comment was as classic Phil as it gets.

I need a drink!!!

Off we went upstairs where it was time for some cognac. Obviously he was thrilled, but the drink was more for his nerves than it was celebration. He asked if I wanted to stay for lunch, but after a drink and about twenty minutes I got home as soon as I could to share the news with my mom.

As was her routine, she eagerly greeted me after every successful check up. Unaware of the surprise that awaited her, from the look on my face she could sense something.

What?

Dr. Brower told me something today.

I know it was wrong not to come out and tell her right away but I couldn't help myself.

What?

What's the matter?

Nothing, he told me I'm cured!

There it was, and with that her face turned as bright red as it had eleven years prior on that day I lay on the couch staring at her as she delivered my fate. Once again I was witnessing tears of joy and they were just as powerful as I had remembered. As I had done with my dad about an hour earlier I now comforted my mom. Just as my dad and I had done, she and I hugged as if letting go wasn't an option. We were in the entry way of the apartment this time around as opposed to the living room but that didn't change the pureness of the moment. We cried together as we had done once before.

OH THANK YOU!

This is the greatest news ever!

I love you so much!!!

I love you too, Ma!

Both my parents were clearly elated but each moment that I spent with them respectively was as far as the celebration went. We didn't talk about it after that and crazy enough they don't even remember me telling them. All they know and want to keep knowing is that I'm healthy. My best friend Durwin on the other hand bought a cake and gathered my friends to celebrate upon learning the news. When I told my folks about this my dad said "Tell Durwin to save his money, we don't need a fuckin' cake. Don't make a big deal, let's just be happy you're healthy and that's it." We did wind up having that cake and I appreciated my friends gathering on my behalf as I remembered a time when they weren't around and I substituted the Tidy Bowl Man and my Joy Juice in their place. We kept the celebration modest but in the end the cake was ice cream and it had crunchies and you know how I feel about that.

Despite the fact that I agree with my folks not to make a big fuss, my belief that kids should never get sick is even stronger. I think it's the cruelest game out there and if I can help put a smile on another kids face and make them forget their reality for a moment the way I did for myself then that's absolutely my obligation and pleasure. Each year I spend time with a group of young children all of whom have severe forms of cancer and one child's presence has remained etched in my memory ever since. He was young, around three and had just had brain surgery days before as his head was still swollen and staples were fresh. I tried to engage him and asked if he wanted to play, talk, whatever. With each request I received a resounding NO. Then I paused, looked at his face, expressions and body demeanor and realized the pain he was in. The two of us had different types of cancer and he was much younger but I had been there. I was the king of one word answers when I was sick and momentarily didn't recognize they were a sign that he wanted to be left alone. Once I did, I took a step back to give him the space he so deserved and had earned and said "No worries." I talked to myself out loud as I walked away.

It's okay little man.

You don't have to do shit.

I get it!

Moments later, one of my friends found me against the wall in the hallway crying. He never knew I was sick and was shocked to find out as we often played basketball together. I told him despite the fact that that little boy was so much younger than me when I was sick I had just seen myself in him. I remembered not wanting to do anything and feeling the way he looked that day. It hit me so deeply that his face has been embedded in my thoughts ever since. It's absolute bullshit that any child should have those days.

I did have them and pray I never have them again but with that said, having cancer and its consequences has made me infinitely stronger both mentally and consequently physically. To put it mildly, you go through ALOTTA shit mentally while undergoing chemo. It tests you in ways you could have never imagined as you literally watch yourself fall apart gradually and inch towards death in a matter of months and quite frankly, it fucks with you. You spend so much time by yourself with nothing to do but think about the "what ifs," it could drive you insane. When you pass by a mirror, you're shocked by the image staring back. "That can't be me" you think to yourself, but it is and there's no escaping that reality. Even when I tried to avoid mirrors altogether there were the reminders. The hair on your pillow, your blackened veins, the pimple rash, the gout, the headaches, the vomiting, the pills, your weight, the dehydration, your white blood count (WBC) or lack thereof causing you to get infections, your collapsed lung that causes you to stutter breath in order to get enough air...the list is endless. There's absolutely no escaping the harshness of your circumstances. You're sick. Really sick!

If and when you're **Fortunate** enough to make it through all of that you come to the realization that there's absolutely nothing in this world that you can't accomplish as everything has to be easier as a result.

When I want to accomplish something and someone says to me "Do you know how difficult what you want to do is going to be?" I often smile and laugh as that same difficulty is my good fortune. Regardless of how "difficult" that something may be, there's no way possible it could prove as cruel as what I've already endured. In actuality it's my pleasure simply having the opportunity. It was all these obstacles and side effects that led me to walk onto the football team at Temple. Why not? What did I have to lose? Yeah, technically I stunk but so what? I had never played organized football a day in my life and I got to experience the sport on a Division I level. Was I the worst player on the field? Absolutely, but you couldn't out work me and I know that drove some of my detractors crazy. They definitely couldn't understand why I kept showing up but how could they? If any of them read this book, maybe they'll finally get it. So what if I got yelled at by a coach or got hit by defender. What could they possibly do to me that was worse then what I had been through? Absolutely nothing!!! Whether good or bad, this "you can't faze me" attitude extends to almost every aspect of my life.

I recall one of my football coaches saw me at the ball for his fraternity. The next day, he said "I saw you at the ball last night. Are you thinking of joining?" On Temple's campus, it was probably a thought most everyone had at least for a minute or two. Then that coach went on to say "Why don't you write me a one page essay on why you're good enough to join the frat." My response? "Why don't you write me a one page essay on why they're good enough to have me join." Needless to say I did a lot of extra running that afternoon at practice. Who cared? I didn't. Hadn't he gotten the memo that to me being at practice was gift? There he was yelling at me unmercifully giving himself a sore throat while probably thinking he was getting the better of me when all along he was doing me a favor. His mind was too weak to understand otherwise. Then again, he wasn't blessed with chemo-power.

Chemo-power

What's that you ask? Chemo-power? Obviously it's not an official medical term but I have to suspect other chemo patients have experienced the phenomenon. There is this calming presence about some of the other chemo patients I have met that people have told me I possess. Very rarely do I get rattled. Even when I've been in the "weeds" (a service industry term for being slammed with customers) when I used to work at one of my restaurants that I now co-own with my dad, more often than not I remained relaxed. At the end of the day, even though myself, my folks or my sister would never have said it then, chemo and cancer was simultaneously the best and worst thing that ever happened to me. It has educated me more than any classroom could ever dream up. There aren't enough power point slides to list the lessons the Big C has taught me. I enjoyed life before but I have become a true life enthusiast.

Prior to getting sick I grew up going to and working at a sleepaway camp. Obviously, I wasn't able to join my friends at camp when I was sick, however, I did return as soon as I was able and Chemo Power became the stuff of lore amongst some of my camp friends. Every summer the staff would have a soccer game that to us was huge deal. I was far from a soccer player but being able to run and potentially kick a ball made me eligible. Long story short, this soccer game was my first athletic event that I was able to take part in since I had gotten sick and I ran and ran like an animal let out of its cage which led me to scoring the winning goal. When I did, my good buddy Ryo (Re-O) and I began celebrating and screaming "Chemo Power!!!" The game ended and since everyone knew my story, both teams left the field gloriously. It's a story Ryo reminds me of to this day.

After business school, I recall interviewing for a position with one of the big banks and the interviewer told me before I made a decision I should know that for the next two or three years I would probably be miserable and would most likely have to sleep in the office a couple nights a week. That person didn't know my medical background, but when I thanked him and we shook hands I informed him that unfortunately I had been miserable before and I had no plan on going back.

Sperm Bank Revisited

Going to a sperm bank was an interesting experience. It was quite possibly one of the funniest shared moments of my life. However, the sperm bank and my "donations" represent an interesting connection to a tough time. They are the one piece of me that remains intact and unscathed from my journey. Those frozen tadpoles are the only thing that didn't get affected by cancer and chemo. At the time they represented the optimism of a robust healthy life as an adult that existed off in the distance. Even though off in the distance has arrived, my tadpoles remain frozen in time. Despite being healthy, Dr. Brower always said I should keep them until I have my kids. When I do have children, beyond the fact that my mom will be thrilled, what will it feel like not to need those sperm anymore? Over the years, it's provided comfort knowing they were there. Will disposing of them be the turning of a final page of a chapter of my life? Time will tell.

Cancer Beyond Being Cured

Having come through my journey, there are the physical scars that everyone can see and the emotional ones they can't. Each day, I live with cancer despite being cancer free. Shhhh… Don't tell my folks I said that! I'm not celebrating, I'm just stating. In the time that has passed since my journey has "officially" ended, my zest for life has caused me to want to do just about everything. Having modeled a bit while I was in college, after I finished grad school, I packed a small bag for Milan where I had been scheduled to model for a week. About six months later I returned with command of a language and incredible affection for my Sicilian family. Upon arrival back in the States I decided to join my dad in the restaurant business and currently I'm his partner in a few Manhattan establishments. Fashion and marketing have always held an enjoyable place in my heart and I've been fortunate to work on some incredible projects for Nike since my return from Milan. Even more special, I have been blessed to work with my best friend Durwin as a behind the scenes partner in the menswear brands Public School and Black Apple which he created. However, the body of work in which I'm most proud, is the one you're currently reading.

Writing a book is an interesting process. Despite the fact that I have always known certain things about myself, there is something to be said for penning it to paper and having it stare back at you. When it does, it's almost as if I added validity to those things as once I put them out there I couldn't take them back. It's been quite humbling actually. Best of all however, is perhaps my words and efforts will help someone else traveling down the same road from which I came. There is life beyond the Big C, I just never knew that its imprint would help shape it the way it has. Then there's Joy Juice the foundation. As I mentioned, I think it's horrible that kids get sick and I hope Joy Juice is able to provide smiles to sick kids and their parents worldwide the way it did for me.

Reflection/Epilogue

Looking back at my time with chemo and cancer I've had two choices. Pretend it never happened or embrace it. I've chosen the latter as there were so many life affirming aspects about my journey. My family and I were afforded second and third chances while some patients never get so lucky. When I think about these chances I have been given they evoke a great deal of sentiment. There were countless times while writing that I cried as intensely as the day each individual event occurred. However, none of these outpours occurred while I was writing solely about myself. Instead, every time they did, it was while writing about my sister, Dr. Brower or my parents.

My sister

You were my first friend, teammate and my biggest fan. As an infant, if I reached for something you got it for me. You anticipated my every move and was there each crawl and step along the way. As kids we did everything together. Rode bikes, played catch and of course every Easter you dressed me up as the Easter bunny. With the experience that comes with being the big sister, you offered encouragement and guidance regardless of what task I faced as you had been there before. Homework, fashion, friends, pressures, you had walked the road. That theory stood the test of time until time seemed to change with that one phone call on that one day. That one day when mommy called you to give you the news. Your baby brother had cancer. Damn, you hadn't been there before. As your little brother you were my all knowing big sister but what wisdom could you impart this time?

It wasn't until ten years or so after my journey began that I had a clear enough head to think about my journey from your perspective. After all, it was your journey too. Just because you were away at school didn't make it any less so. As helpless as mommy and daddy felt you surely felt the same but who could you tell? Me? Probably not. I was blind to the severity of our circumstances so why risk clueing me in. Who's shoulder did you get to lean on? Did my circumstances force you to grow up faster than you were ready for and serve as mommy's pillar of strength since she was distraught and searching for both answers and comfort? Where was your support? Mommy and daddy were beside themselves and their pinpoint focus on me consumed them but did it simultaneously overwhelm you? Twenty-one was just as pivotal an age as seventeen so what about all the issues you were facing? Did you feel left out and alone? I'm sorry for getting sick as I know it was unfair to you.

My sister; we have our own lives now but let me be clear you are still my first friend, teammate and I am **YOUR** biggest fan. I am in awe of your strength and conviction. When I grow up I hope to be just like My Big Sister! I love you!

Dr. Brower

"Oh Captain, My captain!" When my family and I met you what seems like a life time ago you initially knew us only as a referral and instead of treating us like a statistic you did so compassionately. That was your way. You made my parents and me feel as if we were the only patients that mattered. On my longest treatment days I recall seeing patients in the office still waiting for their doctor when I would reemerge. They had been there from the time I arrived. What kind of doctor could keep a sick patient waiting for hours in order to receive their chemo? When I had to visit another doctor, my parents and I were dumbfounded when they made us wait over an hour. You would never have done that to me or any of your patients. As time progressed we developed a relationship closer to father and son as opposed to that of a doctor and patient. You saved my life and for that I am eternally grateful.

This past December of 2012 when I called the office to ask you a question, Laura broke the news to me that you had been killed. What? How do you react when you find out that the man who saved your life has died? In disbelief I called my parents immediately. They were shocked! How could this be? At the time I was putting the finishing touches on the one person show I was writing about my journey which I was dedicating to you. Refusing to believe it was true I sat back down at my computer to reread the section I had written prior to calling Laura. It said "In dedication to Dr. Brower, the man that saved my life." In that instant I realized I had to change those words to "In memory of." That thought hit me so hard I began shaking and crying uncontrollably.

On the day of your service I learned that you had been run over by a taxi cab. Are you fucking kidding me? How could God allow a man that saved thousands of lives be killed by a damn taxi? Where was the justice in that? The rabbi said it was alright to be mad at God for taking you away. Well I am mad and I know from all the kind notes written by so many of your patients so are they. At your service that day, I remember listening to one of your sons talk about how difficult it was when they lost their first patient and you comforted him by saying it was difficult because he was one of the good ones.

He had obviously learned from the best. Then your other son talked about playing catch with you as a child and I couldn't help but think about playing catch with my dad as a boy. I know how I regarded you so I can't even imagine their loss.

It's crazy, I've made a handful of references to "Seinfeld" in my writing only to learn that you had cared for his family and friends as well. From the obituary the Seinfeld's wrote about you in the New York Times it was no surprise they loved you the same as I did. You were beyond my doctor, you were my friend and society is truly less off without you. You are dearly missed and I am honored to have known you. I love you Dr. Brower.

My parents

In the end, my journey as I call it, although its effects continue to resonate through me, still had a much more profound effect on both of my parents than it did on me. Having cancer changed my life and its challenges and triumphs as you now know are a big part of who I am today. My parents on the other hand lived it in a way I could never imagine which if you're a parent you can understand. They've always regretted not getting a sonogram when I hurt my abdomen a year prior to getting my "flu." I can't tell you how many times they've said "If we had only gotten that sonogram when you hurt yourself." Yes the road would have been easier but would we have been as fortunate as we are today? Not that I wish to repeat it, but I'd never take it back. As a family we came together and I believe we are closer and stronger because of it. Regardless of that fact, whenever discussing any part of my being sick both my parents have a limited threshold before the emotions become too great to handle. No matter how healthy I am and how much time passes they can't escape the reality that tortured them. Well mom, dad, I know you don't believe in celebrating and I'm not doing that, but you did it! You dedicated your lives to making sure I would keep mine and I am eternally grateful. You are the reasons I am even capable of writing this book and I hope both it and I make you proud. You are the two greatest gifts I have been given in my life and I owe everything to you. I can't thank you enough. Your baby boy is ok! I love you!!!

Acknowledgements

Mrs. Loutin. You may have passed a long time ago but this book is proof that your diligence not only paid off but resonates today. Every Monday for years, you patiently helped me with my writing. Thank you for your kindness as my stubbornness surely must have tested your patience. I am forever grateful.

Chuck. Under your tutelage, you provided me with the foundation that enabled me to succeed athletically upon arrival at Temple University. I couldn't have done it without you. I'm honored to know you and be your friend! Thank you!!!

Debbie. You are a true friend. I've joked around and called you my gym mom because you have a son named Daniel. When I told you of my nickname for you, you told me only my mom deserved to be called mom and I should call you my aunt. You have been like an angel on my shoulder continuously trying to connect a dot and help me in any way you can. I honestly can't thank you enough.

Every technician. Throughout my journey I have possibly met a hundred technicians (if that's even the correct word), that helped me in some form along the way. I was so fortunate to meet all of you as you each treated me with grace. You enabled a difficult journey to be more palatable and my family and I are eternally grateful.

Don't remember your name. When I started going to Queens College, the office of disabilities introduced me to a young lady whom I used to speak with about being sick. She had Hodgkin's as well except she had stage four as opposed to three/four which I had and what sounds like a slight difference was actually a huge deal. When we thought I needed a bone marrow transplant, she talked to me about the procedure as she had had two. Your spirit was incredible and I'm embarrassed I don't remember your name. For a period of time we spoke every ten days or so. Then one day the phone calls stopped. All too familiar what that could have meant, I didn't have the heart to call your house to see if you were alright. I hope that you are okay and if by chance you read this book, thank you for sharing your experience with me.

Dr. Goldberg. Over the years, you have been a true friend to my family and you helped comfort my parents at the beginning of the most difficult of times. You recommended Dr. Brower because if I were your son that was who you would have sent him to. I want to thank you for your compassion and continued guidance and care. You are truly appreciated.

Dr. Brower. What else can I say? My family and I mourn your tragic loss. It still makes no sense to me. From the bottom of my heart, thank you for everything you did for me and my family. Your compassion and concern for us was unparalleled. Thank you!!!

Laura. There aren't enough words and thanks for everything you've done for me and my family. We wouldn't have been able to make it through without you. For years, you and the office on 61st street were the other part of my social life as I would spend my off days with you in the office when I was capable. I spent so much time in that office I think Dr. Brower was ready to hire me. Truly, thank you!

Cousin Billy. I'm sure I thanked you then but you need to know the sneakers you brought me when I was in the hospital meant the world to me that day. It's the feeling that I want to share with sick kids everywhere and will serve as the core of Joy Juice the foundation. You have always been the big brother I never had and I hope I can be as successful in all aspects of life as the example you have provided for me. Thank you!

Temple University. There aren't enough thanks to express my gratitude to everyone from the faculty, staff, cafeteria, teammates, coaches and friends that all helped make my stay at TU incredible. All of you helped me regain my life and I am forever grateful. We are Temple Made which makes us family. Owls Are Everywhere!

Jen. I'm so glad the duet we created as kids didn't become a solo. You've always looked out for me and even though you're my big sister, it has been incredible watching you become the person you are. I hope I can mirror the strength and conviction in my everyday life that you make look so effortless in yours. Including me, you inspire everyone around you to be better. Thank you for being there for me through everything. I'll never forget that look on your face as you watched them take the tubes out of my lungs. Your support of myself, daddy and especially mommy during our journey is as much a reason for us getting through it as anything else. I'm so proud to be your brother. I love you!

Mom. There is no one like you. You gave me life and I've definitely given you the biggest headache imaginable. Your support over the years has been unwavering. Without your willingness to expose your own emotion and share all the behind the scenes dialogue with doctors and daddy, I would never have been capable of writing this book. One afternoon while writing, you said to me "If there's anything you want to know feel free to ask." "Want to know? I was there. I know what happened." I guess that swagger that I referred to earlier hasn't left my side. It was at that moment in your kind motherly way that you schooled me as to how much about my process I was actually clueless to. Honestly I was flabbergasted! Despite the amount of years that have passed, you still couldn't hold back the emotion as you described your feelings upon receiving countless phone calls or more specifically that day when Dr. Katz delivered those words for the first time.

After gently putting me in my place, from that day forward, every time I had a question I would pick up the phone and you would clue me in. Even though we were on the phone that day we talked about how you felt when you heard Dr. Katz say those words, we shared a moment similar to that winter day on the living room couch during my senior year of high school. One of the things cancer has taught me is that being a parent and the emotion that accompanies it is eternal. Again, it wasn't until I started writing about my journey that I even thought about these particular moments. Doing so has made me realize that moms are often presented with some of the most difficult situations. You have left me in awe of your continued strength and I'm privileged to be your son. I love you!

Pop. You're my dad, brother and best friend all rolled into one. We've shared some amazing times both good and bad and one thing we've learned together is that tough times go away but tough people don't. You've always taught me never to give up and "Keep swinging the bat." It's because you and mommy didn't give up on me that I'm still here able to write these words to you. Two summers ago when I shot that pilot which had big network potential, they interviewed you for your thoughts about me and our time when I was sick. When I mentioned they gave me the outtakes, you told me "Watch those when I'm gone." Well I watched them and I was blown away by your thoughts about me. You said that you were in awe of me because I never complained the entire time that I was sick and that I was your inspiration. While talking about it, you had to take a time out because the emotion was too intense. Despite being ready to "change the fuckin' subject," you put your feelings aside and continued with the interview because you knew that project had the potential to help me. Me…your inspiration? Pop you inspire me every day of my life and everything I achieve is because you and mommy sacrificed the world to give me the opportunity. You are my one true "Captain." I love you!!!

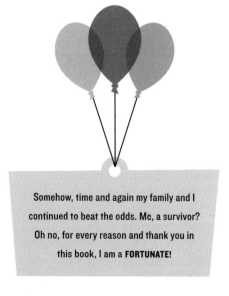

Somehow, time and again my family and I continued to beat the odds. Me, a survivor? Oh no, for every reason and thank you in this book, I am a **FORTUNATE!**

Photo Album

Me and my sis when we were "Brownie Puppies." She's been looking out for me since day one.

My complexion, hair and overall appearance before chemo changed everything.

My first big race. A couple weeks before my diagnosis.

Chemo stripped away my complexion, hair and overall confidence despite remaining upbeat.

Fresh out of the hospital from my laparotomy and after nine months of chemo, I was still holding on to that mess above my lip that drove my sister crazy!

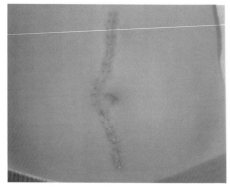

I was so proud to sport my tux at the prom.

My stainless steel midsection

My Queens College ID.

Once my hair grew back, you couldn't tell me anything!

TU gave me my life back. Undoubtedly the greatest place to spend my college days!

Okay, he finally trimmed that mess above his lip but will somebody please tell that boy to cut his hair!

Partners in Crime for life. Me and Durwin. From color guard to the night Public School won the CFDA Award.

Me modeling in Milan

"Tell Durwin to save his money, we don't need a fuckin' cake!" The cake that caused all the fuss.

Me today. Forever the big kid at heart. I guess my Joy Juice has kept me young.

My mom and pop never stopped believing that we would make it "down the road." Their dedication made graduation day at Temple possible. They are the true reasons why today I call myself a **Fortunate.** *I love you!*